DATA
ANALYSIS
FOR
DEVELOPMENT

DATA ANALYSIS FOR DEVELOPMENT

By

ROBERT KLITGAARD

with the assistance of members of
the Applied Economics Research Centre of
the University of Karachi

UGC Monograph Series in Economics

KARACHI
OXFORD UNIVERSITY PRESS
OXFORD   NEW YORK   DELHI
1985

Oxford University Press

OXFORD LONDON

NEW YORK TORONTO MELBOURNE AUCKLAND
KUALA LUMPUR SINGAPORE HONG KONG TOKYO
DELHI BOMBAY CALCUTTA MADRAS KARACHI
NAIROBI DAR ES SALAAM CAPE TOWN

and associates in

BEIRUT BERLIN IBADAN MEXICO CITY NICOSIA

OXFORD is a trademark of Oxford University Press

© Robert Klitgaard, 1985

ISBN 0 19 577313 6

The publisher is grateful to the Ford Foundation for their
assistance in the production of this book.

Typeset by
Industrial Printing Press Ltd.
Printed at
Shaheen Packages, Karachi
Published by
Oxford University Press
5-Bangalore Town, Shara-e-Faisal
P.O. Box 13033, Karachi-8, Pakistan.

CONTENTS

PREFACE

Learning theorists have shown that we learn better from examples than from abstract presentations. In the study of statistics and econometrics, there is no substitute for an adequate theoretical understanding but there is also a great need for examples of statistical tools in action.

The kinds of examples matter. Simple applications of routine statistical tests to hypothetical problems have a limited value. For students in countries like Pakistan, examples drawn from the industrialized West, even if they are realistic and detailed, may have analytical merit but may seem irrelevant. The ideal example would have substantive and not just statistical interest, would refer to the local environment, and would give the flavour of how statisticians analyse data in the messy, imprecise, but exciting 'real world'.

This volume provides such examples of data analysis, all drawn from work at the Applied Economics Research Centre of the University of Karachi. The statistical methods employed include simple and multiple regression, analysis of variance, and factor analysis. The issues examined include fertilizer use and distribution, university grading policies, the determinants of length of life in various countries, secondary schools in Karachi, teacher training, university admissions policies, and the causes of inflation in Pakistan. The attempt is to show how statistical tools are used to help solve real problems.

Five of these examples deal with educational topics. As in the other chapters, the primary purpose is to illustrate concretely the application of statistical and econometrical techniques. There is no effort to prescribe policies. In particular, the reader should not suppose that the book is, in any way, a treatment of the Pakistani educational system. And since all the educational examples are drawn from Karachi, the results may not hold for other parts of Pakistan. Especially students of empirical analysis should be sensitive to the perils of over-generalization.

The chapters stress the exploratory nature of applied data analysis. Regression analysis is a widely used technique, but in many practical applications the analyst cannot be sure that the technique's assumptions are met. Several of the chapters emphasize studying the residuals from a series of regressions as a means of checking the validity of the assumptions and of improving predictions. Throughout the book, the emphasis is on statistical tools as ways to explore data sets, to propose models, and to try to find out what the data may be saying—rather than seeing statistical tools as ends-in-themselves or as strict tests of already proposed theoretical models.

The book should be useful to students of statistics, econometrics, public policy, business administration, education, and the many other fields where data analysis is becoming increasingly important. It is hoped that the book will be a valuable supplement to textbooks of statistics and econometrics, by illustrating the creative possibilities and many pitfalls of real-life applications. Policymakers and policy analysts in government and business should also find much of interest here. With the rising use and importance of surveys, programme evaluation, and other forms of quantitative analysis of social problems, a working knowledge of applied statistics is valuable. One volume will not provide that knowledge, but we hope that the examples provided here will help.

Most of the research reported here was funded by the Ford Foundation, whose support is gratefully acknowledged. John Bresnan, Frank Miller, John Cool, Robert Shaw, and Peter Geithner deserve special thanks. Dr. Ehsan Rashid, the first Director of the Applied Economics Research Centre, encouraged applied statistical and econometrical work and provided leadership in many other ways. Dr. Hafiz Pasha and Dr. Ashfaq Kadri have directed the Centre's activities more recently, and they have emphasized the importance of publishing the Centre's research for a wider audience. All deserve thanks.

Robert Klitgaard
Associate Professor of Public Policy,
John F. Kennedy School of Government, and
Special Assistant to the President,
Harvard University.

CHAPTER 1

THE DETERMINANTS OF THE LENGTH OF LIFE IN ASIAN, AFRICAN AND LATIN AMERICAN COUNTRIES

Frequently social scientists and policy analysts examine cross-sectional data sets using regression analysis. How can the analyst tell which regression model fits the data best? This chapter introduces multiple regression analysis. It illustrates how the analyst can examine histograms, correlation matrices and plots of residuals to assess a regression model. Finally, it provides elementary examples of the interpretation of regression coefficients.

All men are mortal, but in some countries the life expectancy is less than one-third of a century and in others it is well over sixty years.

This study examines seventy-one countries of Asia, Africa, and Latin America to see whether the life expectancy (L/E) in these countries can be predicted with the help of per capita GNP, daily per capita consumption of calories, population density, degree of urbanization of a population, and climatic conditions.

The primary purpose of the analysis is to demonstrate exploratory regression analysis, using a real data set. As we shall emphasize in our conclusions, our findings will be suggestive but will stop far short of direct policy relevance. In particular, we will not be able to give advice about which policy interventions have the greatest effects on life expectancy.

The Data

We took data from F. Harbison, *et al., Quantitative Analysis of Modernization and Development* (1970), as shown in Table 1.1. These are the kinds of variables often used in scholarly studies of development. But each variable has its

---

This chapter was written by Sadequa Dadabhoy and Robert Klitgaard.

Table 1.1
DATA ON SEVENTY-ONE ASIAN, AFRICAN
AND LATIN AMERICAN COUNTRIES

	L/E^1	X_1 p.c. GNP^2	X_2 Cal^3	X_3 Density ^{4}	X_4 % Urban ^{5}	X_5 Temp. rainy ^{6}	X_6 Trop. rainy ^{7}
Afghanistan	45	66	1,950	24	2.7	0	0
Algeria	65	213	2,347	5	13.9	0	0
Angola	45	168	2,170	4	11.5	1	0
Bolivia	46	150	1,860	3	19.4	0	1
Brazil	61	226	2,850	10	28.8	0	1
Burma	48	60	2,320	38	10.4	1	0
Cambodia	48	118	2,040	35	12.1	0	1
Cameroon	38	104	2,130	12	7.0	0	1
Chile	62	490	2,660	12	52.8	0	0
China	68	219	2,400	365	62.0	1	0
Colombia	62	267	2,200	17	31.4	0	1
Congo (Brazzaville)	38	169	2,260	3	15.4	0	1
Congo (Kinshasa)	39	58	2,120	7	16.3	0	1
Costa Rica	65	370	2,460	31	24.0	0	1
Cuba	62	305	2,827	70	42.8	0	1
Ecuador	56	187	1,830	19	26.9	0	1
El Salvador	56	256	2,120	147	17.7	0	1
Ethiopia	41	56	2,040	19	3.7	1	0
Gabon	45	380	1,880	2	15.1	0	1
Ghana	39	220	2,160	34	12.4	0	1
Guatemala	49	291	2,320	43	15.9	1	0
Guinea	30	79	2,170	15	3.6	0	1
Haiti	49	64	2,160	165	5.1	0	1
Honduras	50	209	2,070	22	11.6	0	1
Hong Kong	70	533	2,850	3,708	73.2	1	0
India	45	86	1,810	156	13.9	0	1
Indonesia	47	91	1,980	74	14.9	0	1
Iran	51	232	1,890	16	27.0	0	0
Iraq	54	240	2,100	19	19.9	0	0
Israel	72	1,111	3,450	129	77.9	1	0
Ivory Coast	35	233	2,290	12	13.9	0	1
Jamaica	69	437	2,240	171	24.9	0	1
Japan	71	826	2,350	270	75.5	1	0
Jordan	52	212	2,190	22	22.8	0	0
Kenya	45	89	2,160	17	4.8	0	1
Korea (Republic)	58	139	2,390	302	47.9	0	1
Laos	50	67	2,040	12	10.1	1	0
Lebanon	60	455	2,720	242	53.8	0	1
Liberia	48	200	2,200	10	9.2	0	1
Libya	57	614	2,340	1	23.9	0	0

	L/E^1	X_1 p.c. GNP^2	X_2 Cal^3	X_3 $Density^4$	X_4 % $Urban^5$	X_5 Temp. $rainy^6$	X_6 Trop. $rainy^7$
Malaysia	61	269	2,400	65	20.8	0	1
Mexico	63	443	2,680	23	34.7	1	0
Morocco	53	162	1,980	32	18.8	0	0
Mozambique	45	95	2,420	9	4.4	0	1
Nepal	45	65	2,030	75	2.5	0	0
Nicaragua	50	311	2,550	14	23.0	0	1
Nigeria	41	78	2,180	67	9.0	0	1
Pakistan	45	85	2,290	113	10.3	0	0
Panama	65	488	2,280	18	33.1	0	1
Paraguay	60	196	2,520	5	16.8	0	1
Peru	59	307	2,230	10	28.9	1	0
Philippines	55	151	1,950	116	14.2	0	1
Puerto Rico	72	1,064	2,320	303	27.9	0	1
Rhodesia	52	209	2,450	12	13.9	1	0
Sierra Leone	48	139	2,120	34	6.5	0	1
Singapore	68	544	2,400	3,367	62.7	1	0
Somalia	40	48	1,780	4	7.6	0	0
South Africa	55	530	2,820	15	32.9	0	0
Sri Lanka	62	147	2,180	179	9.7	0	1
Sudan	40	94	1,940	6	4.9	0	0
Syria	52	173	2,600	30	34.3	0	0
Tanzania	41	71	2,808	13	2.5	0	1
Thailand	68	125	2,550	64	16.0	1	0
Togo	35	95	2,170	31	5.3	0	1
Trinidad	69	606	2,920	198	33.8	0	1
Tunisia	53	194	2,390	28	24.4	0	0
Turkey	55	267	3,110	42	21.3	1	0
Uganda	44	96	2,070	34	2.0	0	1
UAE	54	148	2,940	31	22.7	0	0
Uruguay	69	547	3,220	15	61.3	1	0
Venezuela	68	817	2,240	10	47.2	0	1

[1] Life expectancy in years.
[2] Per capita gross national product in dollars.
[3] Per capita daily consumption of calories.
[4] Population density per square kilometre.
[5] Percentage of population in cities over 20,000.
[6] Dummy variable for predominantly temperate, rainy climate.
[7] Dummy variable for predominantly tropical, rainy climate.
Source: F. Harbison, *et al., Quantitative Analysis of Modernization and Development,* 1970; weather data derived by the authors from a climate map in an atlas.

shortcomings. Take life expectancy, for example. It reflects infant mortality as well as mortality that takes place in child-hood or adulthood. Aggregating these may conceal important differences. The socio-economic correlates of infant mortality may be quite different from the socio-economic correlates of adult mortality. Figure 1.1 is a histogram of L/E across countries. The variations are impressive. Of the twenty-five African countries considered, seventeen have an L/E of forty-five years or less. In Guinea the L/E is only thirty years. In Asia, Israel has the highest L/E of seventy-two years, and the other Middle Eastern countries are in the fifty-two to fifty-five years range. Japan and Hong Kong are the other two Asian countries that have an L/E of over seventy years. The countries of the Subcontinent and Afghanistan have an L/E of about forty-five years. Of the Latin and Central American countries considered, Puerto Rico has the highest L/E of seventy-two years. In the countries of Australia, Europe, and North America, the L/E is well over sixty-five years. These countries have not been included in the analysis.

Per capita GNP was another of the variables used in the analysis. It is widely employed as a proxy for the general level of a country's economic development. But it, too, has shortcomings. It does not reflect the distribution of income within a country. It is possible that the majority of a population within one country may be better off economically than the majority of people in another country having a

Figure 1.1
HISTOGRAM OF LIFE EXPECTANCY

Middle of interval	Number of observations	
30	1	*
35	3	***
40	9	*********
45	11	***********
50	13	*************
55	10	**********
60	10	**********
65	3	***
70	11	***********

higher GNP per capita. Figure 1.2 shows the scatterplot of
L/E against per capita GNP.

The other variables we examined were also national
averages, with the same shortcoming of failing to reflect
intracountry variability. Nutritional indicators such as per
capita daily consumption of calories may nonetheless be
useful in assessing the amount of food available. The percentage of a country's population living in urban areas is
interesting because many people believe that urbanization
affects life expectancy. Population density is a related
measure of interest.

As a proxy for geographical and climatic factors two
dummy variables are used. The countries are categorized into
three groups: tropical rainy, temperate rainy, and dry
regions. For instance, a temperate rainy region is given the
values of 1,0; tropical rainy 0,1; and the dry region is
given 0,0.[1]

Figure 1.2
RELATIONSHIP OF LIFE EXPECTANCY TO PER CAPITA GNP

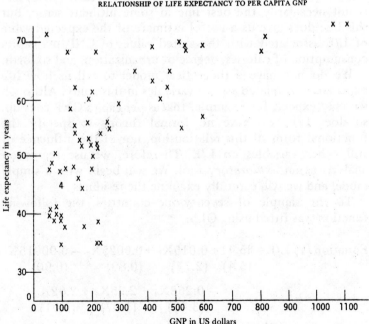

We do not have all the data we would like. We would like to know about other variables: for example, medical infrastructure and the prevalence of various diseases. Even for the variables we have, we would like more detailed data, such as the intracountry distribution of income, calories, and so forth. This lack of complete information is not unusual in studies of developing countries. Indeed, almost every empirical study across countries laments the shortage of available data, as well as the limitations of cross-sectional analysis. Data analysts reside in a world where perfect models and impeccable data do not exist. This fact requires that data analysts be quite modest in the presentation of their findings. It does not mean, however, that the data that are available should not be explored for whatever light they may shed. It is in this spirit that we begin our statistical explorations.

Preliminary Analyses

Regression analysis is a technique for estimating relationships between variables. The ordinary least squares (OLS) line is not necessarily the best line in some ultimate sense. But this line does give us a useful estimate of the expected value of L/E associated with the stated values of GNP, per capita consumption of calories, degree of urbanization, and so forth.

We do not have a theoretical model to tell us how life expectancy is related to the variables in this study. Although we may expect, for example, that as per capita GNP goes up, so does L/E, we have no formal theory to specify the functional form of this relationship, nor of the influence of still other variables on L/E. Therefore, we use regression analysis as an *exploratory* tool. We will begin with a simple model and we will carefully examine the residuals.

To the sample of seventy-one countries, the following function was fitted using OLS:

Equation (1) $L/E = 35.41 + 0.015X_1 + 0.0025X_2 - 0.00015X_3$
$$(5.4) \quad (2.75) \quad (0.80) \quad (0.90)$$

$$- 0.268X_4 + 2.75X_5 + 2.02X_6$$
$$(3.43) \quad (1.07) \quad (1.01)$$

$$\overline{R}^2 = 0.61 \quad \text{S.E. estimate} = 6.69 \quad F = 19.3$$

This is a linear equation. The regression coefficient on X_1 is 0.015, which shows the change in L/E brought about by a one-unit change in X_1, when the other variables are held constant.

Here the variables are:

X_1 = per capita GNP
X_2 = per capita daily consumption of calories
X_3 = population density
X_4 = per cent of population in urban areas
X_5 = temperate rainy country
X_6 = tropical rainy country.

The t-statistics for each regression coefficient are given in parentheses. This statistic tells whether the regression coefficient is significantly different from zero or not. Roughly speaking, if the t-value is greater than about 2, we can reject with 95 per cent confidence the null hypothesis that the regression coefficient is zero. The t-ratio for the constant term, X_1 and X_4 are significant; those for X_2, X_3, X_5, and X_6, are not significant at the $\alpha = 0.05$ level.

The regression explains 61 per cent of the variation in the dependent variable. This is shown by $\bar{R}^2$, which is the ratio of the explained variation to the total variation, adjusted for degrees of freedom.

The standard error of the estimate is 6.69, which is (roughly) the standard error of the predicted L/E for any stated values of X_1 through X_6.

The F-statistic is a summary statistic for the statistical significance of the whole equation. It tells us whether $\bar{R}^2$ is significantly different from zero. In our equation F is 19.3, which is significant at $\alpha = 0.01$. We can say with 99 per cent confidence that the equation is not a random fit.

Examining the Results

OLS regression analysis makes certain assumptions about the nature of the relationships among the variables at hand—and about the error term in the statistical model. For example, it is presumed that the errors are symmetrically distributed and uncorrelated. It is also assumed that the variance of the error term is constant for all values of the independent variables. And, of course, we have assumed a linear, additive equation.

Before we put too much faith in the results of equation (1), we need to examine the extent to which these assumptions are fulfilled in our data set. One way of doing so is to examine the histogram of each independent variable to see if it is symmetrical. The histograms are given in Figures 1.3a-d.

As might have been expected, the histogram of per capita GNP is highly skewed. Most of the countries have a per capita GNP between US$ 100 to US$ 500, with only six countries in the US$ 600 to US$ 1,100 range.

Figure 1.3a
HISTOGRAM OF PER CAPITA GNP

Middle of interval	Number of observations	
0.	1	*
100.	26	*************************
200.	29	*****************************
300.	8	********
400.	4	****
500.	7	*******
600.	2	**
700.	0	
800.	2	**
900.	0	
1,000.	0	
1,100.	2	**

Figure 1.3b
HISTOGRAM OF DAILY PER CAPITA CONSUMPTION OF CALORIES

Middle of interval	Number of observations	
1,800.	6	******
2,000.	13	*************
2,200.	22	**********************
2,400.	14	**************
2,600.	6	******
2,800.	5	*****
3,000.	2	**
3,200.	2	**
3,400.	1	*

The histogram of the daily per capita consumption of calories is also skewed. Most of the countries were within a range of 1,800 to 2,800 calories, with only five countries in the 3,000 to 3,400 range.

The histogram of the per cent of urban population is skewed, too. About 85 per cent of the countries have an urban population comprising only 30 per cent of their total population.

We can also examine the correlation matrix of our predictor variables to get some idea of their interdependence. Although zero-order correlations do not assess all the possibilities of interdependence among variables, they do provide a useful check. Table 1.2 gives the zero-order cor-

Figure 1.3c
HISTOGRAM OF PERCENTAGE OF URBANIZED POPULATION

Middle of interval	Number of observations	
0.	9	*********
10.	21	*********************
20.	19	*******************
30.	11	***********
40.	1	*
50.	4	****
60.	3	***
70.	1	*
80.	2	**

Figure 1.3d
HISTOGRAM OF POPULATION DENSITY PER SQUARE KILOMETRE

Middle of interval	Number of observations	
25.	49	***************************** *******************
75.	6	******
125.	4	****
175.	5	*****
225.	1	*
275.	1	*
325.	2	**
375.	1	*
3,250	1	*
2,750	1	*

Table 1.2
ZERO-ORDER CORRELATION MATRIX

	Per capita GNP	Calories	Population density	Urban population (percentage)
Life expectancy	0.71	0.55	0.32	0.76
Per capita G.N.P	–	0.53	0.25	0.74
Calories	–	–	0.18	0.61
Population density	–	–	–	0.47

relations. Basically, we see little immediate evidence of severe multicollinearity, although the correlation of 0.74 between percentage of urban population and per capita GNP is fairly high. (As a rule of thumb, multicollinearity is not a serious problem unless r = 0.80 or above.)

To examine the assumption of homoscedasticity (error terms with a constant variance), we can plot the standardized residuals against the predicted values of L/E. Does the spread of the residuals get larger (or smaller) with higher predicted L/E? Are there any outliers (observations that do not fit with the pattern of the rest of the data points)? Figure 1.4 gives the plot of standardized residuals from equation (1).

Figure 1.4 shows clear signs of heteroscedasticity. As the predicted L/E goes up, the residuals are less spread out.

Figure 1.4
RESIDUAL PLOT FOR EQUATION (1)

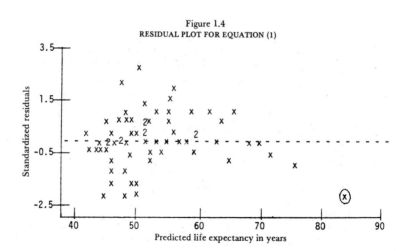

Notice, also, the circled point on the lower right of Figure 1.4. This country (Israel) is predicted by equation (1) to have a life expectancy of well over eighty years, but its actual L/E is 'only' seventy-two years. We will need to consider, in our next steps, whether Israel is to be considered an outlier—that is, a country fundamentally unlike the others in our sample.

The residual plot may also suggest curvilinearity. Although there is no certainty (as with most explorations!), does it seem that the residuals might be falling in an inverted-U pattern? Or is it only the one apparent outlier, Israel, that is responsible for this appearance?

The assumptions of OLS seem to be violated in a number of ways. Remedial actions must be taken, lest our original regression mislead us.

Next Steps

Logarithmic transformations look like a promising remedy for many of equation (1)'s problems. For one thing, they may make the distributions of the independent variables symmetrical. For another, they may reduce zero-order correlations among the independent variables. And it is possible that both heteroscedasticity and our possible outlier may be cured by such transformations.

Moreover, we may be more interested in percentage changes in L/E than in absolute changes, which makes logarithms a good choice for the dependent variable as well.

Figure 1.5a
HISTOGRAM OF LOG_e GNP PER CAPITA

Middle of interval	Number of observations	
4.00	7	*******
4.40	12	************
4.80	7	*******
5.20	16	****************
5.60	12	************
6.00	7	*******
6.40	6	******
6.80	3	***
7.20	1	*

Figure 1.5b
HISTOGRAM OF LOG$_e$ PER CAPITA DAILY CONSUMPTION OF CALORIES

Middle of interval	Number of observations	
7.500	3	***
7.550	4	****
7.600	8	********
7.650	8	********
7.700	15	***************
7.750	9	*********
7.800	8	********
7.850	4	****
7.900	3	***
7.950	4	****
8.000	2	**
8.050	1	*
8.100	1	*
8.150	1	*

Figure 1.5c
HISTOGRAM OF LOG$_e$ PER CENT OF URBAN POPULATION

Middle of interval	Number of observations	
0.50	1	*
1.00	3	***
1.50	7	*******
2.00	5	*****
2.50	17	*****************
3.00	16	****************
3.50	11	***********
4.00	8	********
4.50	3	***

Figure 1.5d
HISTOGRAM OF LOG$_e$ POPULATION DENSITY

Middle of interval	Number of observations	
0.0	1	*
1.0	5	*****
2.0	14	**************
3.0	22	**********************
4.0	13	*************
5.0	10	**********
6.0	4	****
7.0	0	
8.0	2	**

Figure 1.5e
HISTOGRAM OF LOG_e OF LIFE EXPECTANCY

Middle of interval	Number of observations	
3.40	1	*
3.50	0	
3.60	5	*****
3.70	7	*******
3.80	10	**********
3.90	13	*************
4.00	13	*************
4.10	11	***********
4.20	10	**********
4.30	3	***

Natural logs (abbreviated 'ln') of both the dependent and the independent variables were taken. As Figures 1.5a to 1.5e show, these transformations made the skewed distributions almost symmetrical. The histogram of the transformed dependent variable was slightly negatively skewed.

The zero-order correlation matrix of the transformed variables is given in Table 1.3. Once again we find little immediate evidence of severe multicollinearity. The correlation between ln percentage of urban population and ln per capita GNP is 0.79, but for the purpose of the overall predictive power of the equation, we are not too worried about the result.

The transformed variables yielded a new regression equation.

Equation (2) $\ln L/E = 2.61 + 0.096\ln X_1 + 0.06\ln X_2 + 0.034\ln X_3$
$\qquad\qquad\quad (2.61)\quad (2.94)\qquad (0.046)\quad (3.38)$
$\qquad\qquad\quad + 0.08\ln X_4 + 0.04 X_5 - 0.0005 X_6$
$\qquad\qquad\qquad (2.65)\quad\; (0.83)\quad\; (0.01)$

$\bar{R}^2 = 64.5$ per cent   S.E. estimate = 0.124 $F = 22.2$

Table 1.3
ZERO-ORDER CORRELATION MATRIX FOR NATURAL LOGS

	ln Per capita GNP	ln Calories	ln Population density	ln Urban population (percentage)
ln life expectancy	0.72	0.52	0.47	0.75
ln per capita GNP	–	0.56	0.20	0.79
ln calories	–	–	0.25	0.56
ln population density	–	–	–	0.31

The t-ratios indicate that the regression coefficients for $\ln X_2$, X_5 and X_6 are significantly different from zero. That is to say: there is evidence that the log of daily per capita consumption of calories and the dummies for climatic conditions are not significantly affecting the log of L/E, keeping other things equal.

The $\bar{R}^2$ is 64.5 per cent (adjusted for degrees of freedom), which is relatively high, with a small standard error of estimate and a significant F-ratio. Figure 1.6 shows the residual plot from equation (2). Notice that the apparent outlier on the extreme right in Figure 1.4 no longer looks like an outlier. Also, there is now little visual appearance of curvi-linearity.

However, a number of countries were away from the main group: see the circled countries in Figure 1.6. Further examination revealed that these countries were all in Africa. To improve the fit of regression (2), a dummy variable was introduced, which categorized the data into two parts. Those that were African were given the value 1, and all others were given 0. This new variable was called X_7.

The new regression with the above dummy variable included was:

$$\text{Equation(3)} \ln L/E = 2.42 + 0.099\ln X_1 + 0.106\ln X_2 + 0.021\ln X_3$$
$$ (2.63) \quad (3.31) \quad\quad (0.84) \quad\quad (2.2)$$
$$+ 0.05\ln X_4 + 0.021X_5 - 0.01X_6 - 0.121X_7$$
$$(1.75) \quad\quad (0.01) \quad\quad (0.32) \quad (3.51)$$

$$\bar{R}^2 = 69.8 \text{ per cent} \quad \text{S.E. estimate} = 0.114 \quad F = 24.1$$

The t-ratio of X_7 (the African dummy variable) is 3.51, which shows that the variable is significantly influencing the predicted L/E. The negative sign of this variable's coefficient shows that in the case of an African country, the L/E is lower, other things being equal.

The t-ratios in equation (3) indicate that the per capita GNP, population density, percentage of urbanized population, and the dummy variable for African countries are the significant variables affecting life expectancy.

The plot of the residuals versus the predicted values of L/E for equation (3) showed that the observations were within a range of −2.2 to 2.0 with a tapering on the right hand side (Figure 1.7). This could be because of a sort of 'ceiling effect' on L/E in reality. No matter what a country's GNP, one might say, there are biological limits to its citizens' life expectancy. We probably can do little to get rid of this effect in here; the heteroscedasticity is not a statistical artefact.

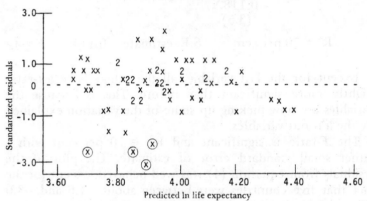

Figure 1.6
RESIDUAL PLOT FOR EQUATION (2)

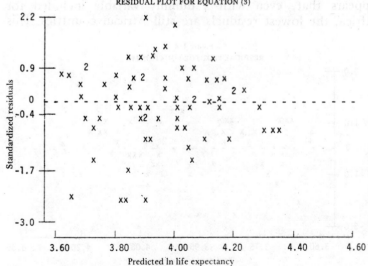

Figure 1.7
RESIDUAL PLOT FOR EQUATION (3)

Looking at the Significant Predictors

A new regression was run using only the four significant variables that affect the L/E in equation (3). These are per capita GNP, population density, percentage of urban population, and the African dummy variable.

$$\text{Equation (4)} \ln L/E = 3.18 + 0.103\ln X_1 + 0.025\ln X_2 + 0.061nX_3$$
$$\quad\quad\quad\quad (27.8) \quad (3.6) \quad\quad (2.5) \quad\quad (2.2)$$
$$-0.118X_7$$
$$(3.5)$$

$$\overline{R}^2 = 70 \text{ per cent} \quad\quad \text{S.E. estimate} = 0.114 \quad F = 42$$

Except for the last variable, all the others have a t-ratio slightly more significant than before. This is because the variables are now picking up some of the variation explained by the left-out variables.

The F-ratio is significant and $\overline{R}^2 = 70$ per cent with a rather small standard error of estimate. The plot of the residuals from equation (4) was well behaved, except for the fact that five countries were between about -1.6 and -3.0 (Figure 1.8). Examination revealed that these were African countries between the range of thirty to thirty-eight years. It appears that, even with a dummy variable included for Africa, the lowest residuals are still African countries. This

Figure 1.8

RESIDUAL PLOT FOR EQUATION (4)

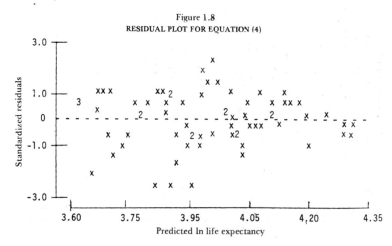

Predicted ln life expectancy

may mean that our dummy variable X_7 has not captured all the effects on life expectancy of being in Africa. It may be a sign that a different functional relationship exists between L/E and the predictor variables in African countries.[2]

Suppose that African countries had equal values of per capita GNP, population density, and percentage of urban population as the rest of the countries in the sample. Then what would the predicted L/E be in African countries, according to equation (4)? Substituting the average figures, L/E would be fifty-three years.

Conclusions

Our study is exploratory in several senses. First, we have tried to find the best combination of a variety of plausible predictors of life expectancy. We had no formal model to guide the choice of variables or the particular functional form that we should use. Since we selected and transformed variables based on goodness of fit, the statistics of the regression equation (such as the *t*-ratios) do not have their usual properties for exact tests of various hypotheses. This need not worry us, as long as we realize that *our objective is to suggest hypotheses, rather than to confirm them.* We are exploring the terrain, trying to find the most promising avenues for further, more detailed research.

Second, as noted earlier, many important variables could not be included in the study, due to a lack of readily available information. Measures of health services, for example, would seem relevant to predicting L/E, but data were not present. Better measures of food quality and consumption, as well as of the distribution of GNP, would also be interesting to examine. Racial and ethnic variables might have predictive power. Our study has been a partial exploration, not a definitive one.

Third, our work is cross-sectional. We have examined many countries at one point in time (most of the data are from the mid-sixties). We have not studied the relationship within countries of changes over time in the predictor variables to changes over time in life expectancy. Neither, of course, do we have anything approximating a controlled scientific experiment with which to assess causation. (Experiments here would probably be unfeasible as well as unethical.)

Nonetheless, we have some interesting and suggestive results from our work.

We have seen that per capita GNP, the degree of urbanization, and population density are associated with life expectancy. In addition, after statistically controlling for these variables, life expectancy in African countries was about 11 per cent less than in the other countries in our sample.

It is perhaps surprising that the daily per capita consumption of calories is not an important independent factor in the prediction of life expectancy. We had anticipated a positive effect of calories on L/E. However, Dr. Grigoriu Pitzelari of the USSR reported to the 1976 International Congress of the Federation for Assistance to Aged Persons that 'a low calorie diet may be part of the secret of long life in Soviet Georgia'.[3]

Our crude proxies for climatic conditions did not show any power in the prediction of L/E. Better measures might yield different results.

What does our study say about Pakistan? In 1970 the average Pakistani lived forty-nine years. By increasing the per capita GNP to the average of our sample, the predicted life expectancy of a Pakistani would be fifty-three years, i.e., an increase of almost 10 per cent. GNP is a proxy for economic development. An increase in per capita GNP usually is associated with better medical facilities and other health benefits, which perhaps explains its association with L/E.

The degree of urbanization is yet another important factor. By raising Pakistan's degree of urbanization to the average of our sample, the predicted L/E would increase by about 8 per cent. We suspect that medical facilities are better in urban areas, thus increasing longevity despite the possible deleterious effects of crowding in cities.

But our sample's average population density is above that of Pakistan. Therefore, by increasing Pakistan's population density to the average level, L/E for Pakistan would be expected to fall by about 4 per cent.

These are, of course, only illustrative results. A study of this kind does not enable firm predictions to be made. But it may suggest that life expectancy is associated with per capita GNP, population density, and urbanization, hypotheses that are worth investigating using other methodologies and data sets.

NOTES

1 The assignment of countries to different categories was crude, but we hope useful. The idea was to classify countries according to the climatic conditions prevailing in the largest geographical area of the country.

2 Or, that a subset of African countries is 'different'.

3 *International Herald Tribune*, 8 June 1976, p. 4.

CHAPTER 2

USING REGRESSION ANALYSIS
TO ASSESS SCHOOL POLICIES*

Multiple regression analysis is also used to estimate in advance
how much difference changes in policy may make. This chapter
presents a decision-oriented case study. The reader is shown a
strategy for building and testing a regression model in a policy
setting. Then comes an even more difficult question: given
the results of a regression study, what can and cannot be conclu-
ded for policymaking purpose?

The Policy Problem

The night was so sultry that even the mosquitoes were lan-
guid. Around the outdoor buffet table a swarm of nattily
clad guests droned on. Mr. P. F. Siddiqui, a researcher at a
local university, sought solitude out on the lawn. The view
was striking. Above the concrete wall topped with serrated
glass, he saw the lights from the huts of half a lakh of people.
That poor human hive now possessed a beauty and an order
that dissólved in squalor with the daylight.

'Good evening, Mr. Siddiqui. I've been looking for you.
Have you a moment?'

It was the voice of Mr. Ibrahim Mula, the Minister of
Education and host of the party. 'I have a terrible problem
on which your advice would be most welcome.'

Siddiqui greeted the Minister and expressed his acquiescence.

'I am certain you have heard about the Chief Minister's
recent gathering', the Minister began. Siddiqui said he had.
Two days before, the Chief Minister had called a large,
private meeting with a hundred of the city's leading citizens,
who were not members or supporters of the party in power.

*This chapter is based on real data from Karachi's public schools in the
mid-seventies. The policy problem is also a real one, although the names are
fictitious and the conversations are stylized. The case offers not only a chance to
see a novel technique of data analysis in action, but also to ponder on what the
results might mean for policymaking.

This chapter was written by Robert Klitgaard. Sadequa Dadabhoy and Simin
Litkouhi provided research assistance.

He had asked them where the government could improve its performance. 'The primary issue they raised, and they spent over an hour haranguing him about it, was the academic quality of our public schools. I am now under great pressure to tell him how my Ministry plans to improve the situation, especially in the secondary schools. But I do not know which school policies, if changed, would raise examinations scores. Can you help me?'

Siddiqui knew that in his country students, parents, teachers, and policymakers all behaved as though examination scores measured educational achievement. The Matric Exams given after tenth grade played an extraordinary role in shaping students' future academic and employment possibilities. Examination scores were the principal criterion for admission to higher educational levels, and jobs often required examination scores above a certain minimum.

'There is no shortage of concerned parties offering me advice', said the Minister. 'Some recommend more teachers, others higher salaries, still others better teacher training. Some of my colleagues, no doubt, would call for all three. But I have few data and almost no relevant analysis.'[1]

Siddiqui explained that even with more data, estimating the effects of school policies was problematical. 'One cannot simply look across schools at the relationship between, for example, the school averages for Matric scores and teachers' salaries. Other factors that influence scores must be taken into account.'

'What do you have in mind?'

'Well, test scores are not influenced only by school policy variables. They also depend on the socio-economic backgrounds and innate endowments of students. For example, students from wealthy families will usually do better than students from poor families. We cannot simply assume that these important determinants of success are randomly distributed across schools. So, we must statistically control for socio-economic variables before the relative importance of school policies can be assessed.'

The Minister looked somewhat puzzled, and his party needed tending. 'Would it be at all possible', he inquired politely, 'for you to drop by my office at six o'clock tomorrow? If so, we might discuss these issues in depth'. Siddiqui agreed. It turned out to be the start of something big.

The Statistical Problem

The next evening Siddiqui spent two hours with the Minister and four members of his research staff. The topic was methodology. Fortunately, all his listeners but one—the Minister himself—were acquainted with the basics of regression analysis.

Siddiqui explained how multiple regression analysis tries to 'control' statistically for the many factors that influence an outcome like examination scores. He said that the Minister should think of a vague model of the form:

scores = f (students' backgrounds, school variables, . . .)

'By controlling for students' backgrounds in a regression equation', Siddiqui argued, 'we might hope to obtain estimates of the effects of various school policy variables on examination scores'.

'Is this an easy task?' asked the Minister.

'Several problems arise, and they strain the frontiers of applied statistics', Siddiqui replied. 'Your policy question, Mr. Minister, leads squarely into a statistical issue of considerable generality.'

'It is a difficulty we often encounter', noted one of the officials, Mr. Akbar, not too convincingly.

'Frequently in regression models applied to public policy', P.F. Siddiqui went on, 'we have no theoretical model to guide statistical testing. Which variables should be used? Should there be interaction terms? Should variables be transformed? Should all observations be used? With a pre-specified regression model, these questions disappear. The form of the regression equation is given, and the statistician's job is to compute the relevant coefficients and test statistics. But without an *a priori* model, we are in trouble.'

'One could simply assume a certain model', noted another official, Mr. Waloo. 'Educational researchers often posit a linear additive model with all variables included. They presume that interactions among the independent variables are non-existent, and that the error term is, unlike most of their students, "well-behaved". This approach is convenient, and if its assumptions are valid, standard techniques yield efficient estimators and exact test statistics.'

'But can the assumptions be defended in real life?' asked Siddiqui rhetorically. 'If reality is not benign, the choice of variables and specifications can make a big difference to the computed coefficients and test statistics. And in complex situations like ours, the usual assumptions are frequently violated. Regression models that assume too much can easily be dead wrong.'[2]

'I quite agree', said Waloo. 'One answer is to forget about theoretical models and go straight to the data. For example, some investigators will run a series of multiple regressions, examine the results, and then make additional runs based on those results. After much statistical massaging, the analyst will choose a "best" regression equation.'

Though somewhat at sea, the Minister was still attentive. Siddiqui and the others were just getting limbered up.

'This sort of exploratory approach has much to recommend it', said Mrs. Sharji with animation. 'But a new problem emerges. The regression statistics derived from the so-called "best" equation—you know, t, F, $\bar{R}^2$, and so forth—are biased upward by the sequential contingent methods used to find that equation. Indeed, these statistics no longer have their usual interpretations.'

'In addition', remarked Waloo, 'there is no criterion for accepting a particular equation as best'.[3]

Mr. Din Muhammed, a thin and scholarly looking man, spoke for the first time. 'A third approach is the formalization of a regression strategy, but for practical purposes it has been of little use. One might hope to analyse the effects of various regression strategies on the test statistics of the final regression equations.'

'What do you mean by a regression strategy?' asked Akbar.

'A regression strategy is a set of instructions given in advance by the analyst. The instructions define what subsequent statistical analyses should be carried out, subject to the information available from the previous analysis. For example, one simple regression strategy would begin with a linear additive model and would delete all independent variables not significant at the 0.05 level. The problem is, even when the error terms are independent normal variates with a constant variance, the bias introduced by relatively straightforward regression strategies cannot be specified. This bias turns out to depend on both the unknown true values of the coefficients and the variance of errors.[4] No one has comprehensively analysed the biases that may be introduced in more complicated strategies—although various authors have shown how much can sometimes be learned by following exploratory strategies.'[5]

The Minister had become restless.

'Before I leave it to you chaps to work it out, tell me this. Can we do a study that will yield useful results for my problem? Or do these problems of method preclude it?'

There was a long pause. Then Siddiqui spoke.

'I have been studying a way out of the statistical dilemma', he said. 'If we have enough data, we can randomly divide them into several parts. For example, we might split the data set in two. We then lock half the data set in a safe and not examine it. We massage, in Mr. Waloo's words, the other half. We try to find a good regression model. Then we test this on the safeguarded half.'[6]

'It sounds very interesting' the Minister said, clearing his throat. 'I beg you, however, to remember the problem the Chief Minister and I, and all of us really, now face. You have my support to undertake this statistical study. But as you design a good study, please do also make it a useful one.'

Siddiqui was hired as a consultant and chief investigator on what turned out to be a path-breaking project. In this country, no one had looked at the effects of school policies in a quantitative way before. Siddiqui cared about improving secondary schools. He also wanted to find out how his approach to the general statistical problem of 'regression without a model' would work out in a concrete case.

The Data

Under Siddiqui's supervision, data were laboriously gathered from a stratified random sample of 208 of the city's 348 secondary schools. Matric scores were obtained for Humanities and Science students. These were separate tracks; students taking Science did not take Humanities tests. Data were compiled for each school on the number of students in ninth and tenth grades; the number of teachers who taught in those grades; the numbers of such teachers holding different educational degrees (B.Ed., M.Ed., and others), having first-class degrees at the B.Ed. level, and having more than five years experience; the percentage of male teachers; and the average salary of teachers. This information was used to calculate for each school the student/teacher ratio and the percentage of teachers having these characteristics of education and experience.

Finally, two sorts of data on the socio-economic characteristics were collected. The city's recent Master Plan included a detailed socio-economic map of the blocks in the city. Each block was classified into one of eight socio-economic categories, one being the lowest, according to an aggregate of four indices: median household income, literacy rate among adults, percentage of dwellings with hard-wall and soft-wall construction, and percentage with water. Based on its location, each school in the sample was assigned to one of the eight categories. (School district officials said that most students attended schools in their immediate neighbourhood.) This variable was called 'SES (region)'.

The second socio-economic variable was based on interviews with knowledgeable school district officials. These officials classified each school according to the average income of the households of its students. There were five categories. Officials ranking the same schools were in close agreement about the classifications. This variable was called 'SES (income)'. Both SES measures were aggregated proxy variables rather than pupil-level direct measurements. After finishing the study, the correlation between SES (region) and SES (income) was computed. It turned out to be 0.42.

Statistical Explorations

After collecting these data, Siddiqui and his colleagues randomly divided the schools into two groups, stratified by SES (region). One half of the data was safeguarded and not

examined. The other half was subjected to numerous statistical analyses. To illustrate both method and findings, their
explorations involving Science test scores are presented in
some detail here, with only a summary of their efforts on
the Humanities scores.

Their first steps on the analysed half involved data editing:
the removal of nonresponses and, occasionally, mistakes in
the data. Several schools did not provide information for
every variable, and in the multiple regressions these schools
were deleted. Schools with five or fewer students tested were
also dropped. School mean examination scores were adjusted
for reliability.[7] The means and standard deviations of
selected variables are given in Table 2.1.

Next, histograms and two-way plots of the variables were
examined for asymmetry and clustering. Because of skewness
in the histograms and curvature in some plots, Siddiqui *et al.*
experimented with logarithmic transformations for student/
teacher ratio, number of students, the percentage of teachers
with experience greater than five years, and teachers' average
salary. The clustering of two variables—the percentage of
teachers with first-division standing in B.Ed. theory and the
percentage with first-division in B.Ed. practical—led them to
try dichotomous variables for each. SES (region) was
collapsed into seven categories: category three was combined
with category two, on the basis of a very small number of

Table 2.1
MEANS AND STANDARD DEVIATIONS FOR
SELECTED VARIABLES, FIRST HALF OF SCIENCE DATA
(N = 79)

Variables' name	Mean	Standard deviations
SES (region)	4.39	1.81
Girls' school (dummy)	0.32	—
Boys' school (dummy)	0.48	—
Government school (dummy)	0.30	—
Nationalized school (dummy)	0.54	—
Student/teacher ratio	15.06	6.34
Percentage of teachers with more than five years experience	66.89	25.73
Average teachers' salary (in rupees)	520.00	91.20
Science score average	437.10	71.50
Science score standard deviation	96.50	21.50
SES (income)	2.54	1.14

observations in three and similar average Science scores to two. In the regressions, these variables were tried in both their new form (that is, at logs or dummies) and their old, untransformed scaling.

The correlation matrix of all untransformed variables was computed and examined (Table 2.2). The absence of strong correlations between the socio-economic variables and school policy variables surprised Siddiqui. (This result is usual in American studies, but he believed that in his country the rich would have much better schools, as measured by these variables.) From a statistical point of view, he was pleased: multicollinearity did not seem a problem.

Then Siddiqui and his colleagues experimented with many and varied multiple regressions, using the average Science score as the dependent variable. Some regressions included all the variables; others included subsets. Residuals from each regression equation were plotted against predicted Science scores and against each independent variable. In the style of exploratory data analysis, Siddiqui looked for visual patterns in the residuals: 'bends' that might indicate curvilinearity, 'fans' that might reveal heteroscedasticity, and 'outliers', or unusual data points, that might distort the regression equation. For example, Figure 2.1 shows a plot of residuals from one of the equations against one of the independent variables, teachers' salary. He thought the plot showed some curvature, and in a future equation, he included salary and (salary)^2 as independent variables. The result was an improved fit, both variables statistically significant, and a homoscedastic residual plot.

The early results indicated that the significant variables were SES (income), SES (region), teachers' salary, and dummy variables for type of school (boys', girls', mixed; government, nationalized, exempted). Siddiqui therefore concentrated on possible transformations of and interactions among them. For example:

- Because of apparent curvature in a residual plot, he tried adding a quadratic term, SES (income)^2, in several of the equations. Its coefficient was not statistically significant, nor did it affect the coefficients of other independent variables much.

Table 2.2
CORRELATION MATRIX FOR FIRST HALF OF SCIENCE DATA

	3	4	5	6	7	8	9	10	11	12	13	14	15	16	17	18	19	
2	-0.06	0.00	-0.11	0.13	-0.07	-0.09	0.25	0.27	0.04	-0.03	-0.05	0.02	0.09	0.20	-0.02	0.43	0.08	2
3		-0.65	0.14	-0.08	0.00	-0.08	0.13	0.13	0.05	-0.72	0.02	0.09	0.07	0.20	-0.10	-0.06	-0.26	3
4			0.08	0.11	0.22	0.31	-0.14	-0.24	0.13	0.72	0.02	-0.18	0.05	-0.43	0.24	-0.24	0.34	4
5				-0.72	0.42	0.18	-0.16	-0.14	0.36	0.18	0.20	0.15	-0.05	-0.02	0.22	-0.29	0.25	5
6					-0.30	-0.01	-0.07	-0.02	-0.26	-0.07	-0.34	-0.14	0.11	-0.03	-0.02	-0.14	-0.24	6
7						0.73	-0.19	-0.16	0.18	0.28	0.11	0.03	0.04	-0.09	0.20	-0.17	0.75	7
8							-0.22	-0.20	0.20	0.33	0.02	-0.22	0.28	0.21	0.24	-0.26	0.58	8
9								0.72		-0.18	0.02	-0.14	0.15	0.16	-0.30	0.28	-0.12	9
10									-0.08	-0.21	-0.08	-0.05	0.00	0.07	-0.18	0.30	-0.12	10
11										0.16	0.10	0.00	0.14	-0.31	0.11	-0.05	0.20	11
12											0.03	-0.06	-0.11	0.31	—	-0.17	0.41	12
13												0.01	-0.06	0.00	-0.21	0.20	0.07	13
14													-0.66	-0.00	0.04	-0.03	0.03	14
15															0.04	-0.03	0.03	15
16															-0.35	0.57	-0.01	16
17																-0.35	0.16	17
18																	-0.02	18

2 = SES (region)
3 = Girls' school
4 = Boys' school
5 = Government school
6 = Nationalized school
7 = Number of students in class IX and X
8 = Student/teacher ratio
9 = Percentage of teachers with first division degrees in B.Ed. (theory)
10 = Percentage of teachers with first division degrees in B.Ed. (practical)
11 = Percentage of teachers with more than five years experience
12 = Percentage of male teachers
13 = Average salary in rupees
14 = Percentage of teachers with M.Ed. degrees
15 = Percentage of teachers with B.Ed. degrees only
16 = Mean Science score
17 = Standard deviation Science score
18 = SES (income)
19 = Number of students passed Science X

- For the same reason, he experimented with an interaction term between salary and SES (income). In
addition to one term for salary and another for SES
(income), he included a term for salary times SES
(income). The coefficient of this interaction term was
not significant, nor did its inclusion greatly affect the
regression coefficients of other variables.
- He recoded the five category SES (income) into three
categories, combining the middle three, but the new
variable's coefficient became insignificant.
- He tried different weightings of the SES (region)
variable, to protect against possible nonlinearity.[8] He
used John Tukey's 'linear two-four' weighting system.
According to Monte Carlo experiments, when marked
nonlinearities are present, this system is about 90 per
cent as good in the sense of R^2 as the complex optimal
weighting system derived by Tukey and others.[9] However, using this system did not improve the regression
results.

Figure 2.1
EXAMPLE OF A RESIDUAL PLOT

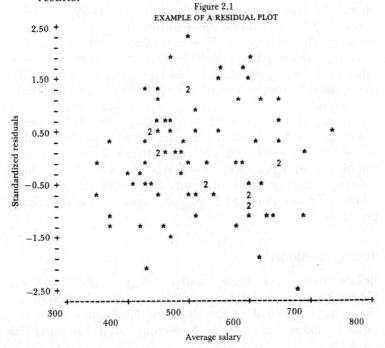

At the end of these and many other explorations, Siddiqui and his co-workers found what they considered to be a preferred regression equation. Its residual plots were well-behaved, and the inclusion of the left-out variables did not greatly alter the equation's predictive power or the regression coefficients. Several results stood out (see Table 2.3, first row).

First, only one policy variable was statistically significant: teachers' average salary. No matter what the functional form and what the included variables, none of the coefficients of other variables relating to teacher characteristics differed significantly·from zero. The curvilinear relationship between salary and Science scores, other things being equal, suggested that salary gains were most important to teachers with low salaries. At the mean of teachers' salaries, a 100-rupee monthly pay increase corresponded to a 146 point increase in average Science achievement. (For the entire data set, the mean Science score was 443 and the standard deviation among school means was 70. The mean salary was Rs 519 and the standard deviation among school means was 89.)

Second, boys' schools did significantly worse than girls' schools. The estimated difference was about 42 points.

Third, private schools had higher average Science scores, other things being equal, as indicated by the negative coefficients on the dummy variables for government and nationalized schools. The difference for nationalized schools was significant at the $\alpha = 0.05$ level, using a one-sided t-test.

Finally, the SES (income) variable was an important predictor of Science scores. The difference between the lowest and the highest SES (income) schools was 21.6 x 4 = 86.4 points, holding other variables constant. Once SES (income) was taken into account, SES (region) was not a significant predictor.

Testing the Model

Before they took these results too seriously, however, Siddiqui and his colleagues tested this preferred equation on the safeguarded half of the data set. The results when the same equation was tried on the second half are summarized

Table 2.3
REGRESSION RESULTS ON SCIENCE SCORES

	Constant	SES		Type of school		Administration		Policy variables		$\bar{R}^2$	S.E. estimate	F
		Income	Region	Girls'	Boys'	Government	Nationalized	Salary	(Salary)²			
1. First half of data set (n = 79)	-25.38 (-0.13)	21.60 (2.76)	3.39 (0.86)	1.59 (0.09)	-40.05 (-2.28)	-15.02 (-0.61)	-41.51 (-1.84)	1.56 (2.12)	-0.001 (-1.93)	0.472	51.93	9.73
2. Second half of data set (n = 84)	420.68 (2.54)	29.44 (3.93)	-1.73 (-0.42)	-0.32 (-0.01)	-41.56 (-1.68)	-27.33 (-1.07)	-17.30 (-0.80)	-0.10 (-0.16)	0.0002 (0.32)	0.392	53.16	7.69

Note: Figures in parentheses are t-statistics. Underlining indicates (one-sided) statistical significance beyond the α = 0.05 level.

in the second row of Table 2.3. The means and standard deviations for the second half are presented in Table 2.4.

The results certainly changed. The most important difference was that the salary variables were no longer significant. Indeed, the regression coefficient on the linear salary term was slightly negative. Based on the second half of the data set alone, a 100-rupee raise in average salary corresponded to an 8-point decline in average Science score. The effect 'discovered' in the detailed explorations with the first half of the data set seemed to have been an artefact of random fluctuation. On the basis of the second half, they could not reject the null hypothesis that the average salary coefficient is zero, using a joint F-test.

The constant term in the new equation was much larger. SES (income) was large and significant: average Science scores in schools of SES (income) category one were 117.76 points lower than in SES (income) category five, other variables held constant. Boys' schools averaged about 41 points lower than both coed and girls' schools, other things being equal, which was almost identical to the finding in the first equation. The coefficient for nationalized schools was no longer significantly negative.

Siddiqui and his colleagues were tempted to conclude that the number of teachers, their educational qualifications, and

Table 2.4
MEANS AND STANDARD DEVIATIONS FOR
SELECTED VARIABLES, SECOND HALF OF SCIENCE DATA
(N = 84)

Variables' name	Mean	Standard deviations
SES (region)	4.43	1.79
Girls' school (dummy)	0.34	—
Boys' school (dummy)	0.59	—
Government school (dummy)	0.23	—
Nationalized school (dummy)	0.62	—
Student/teacher ratio	16.09	8.05
Percentage of teachers with more than five years experience	61.82	26.26
Average teachers' salary (in rupees)	538.10	88.30
Science score average	452.20	63.60
Science score standard deviation	97.70	21.20
SES (income)	2.60	1.11

their salaries were not significantly related to student test performance. But they also analysed the Humanities test scores, and the results of their similar statistical explorations with this dependent variable had to be considered.

In the preferred regression for the first half of the Humanities data, there were some interesting differences from the Science results. SES (income) had a curvilinear relationship to Humanities scores, which seemed to be captured best by including both a linear and quadratic term. Another policy variable, the natural logarithm of the percentage of teachers having a Masters degree, was also significant. However, it had a negative effect on scores. The first row of Table 2.5 presents Siddiqui's preferred regression equation for the first half of the Humanities data.

As in the case of Science scores, the regression on the second half of the data did not fully support the model developed from the first half as Row 2 of Table 2.5 shows. SES (income) turned out not to have a significant curvilinear relationship to Humanities scores; salary was significant in both halves, but not in a curvilinear way in the second; and the surprising negative coefficient on ln percentage of M.Ed. was not significant in the second half. Furthermore, SES (region) was positive and significant in the first half but negative and insignificant in the second.

The results of the Humanities tests, then, tended to support the findings regarding Science scores. SES (income) was the most important predictor. Girls' schools did better than boys' schools. Although this time salary was a significant variable, the coefficient was small. Based on equation 2b, a 100-rupee raise in average salary corresponds to a rise of only about 16 points in average Humanities score. (The mean Humanities score was 382 and the standard deviation of school mean scores was 66.) This variable is statistically significant but may be practically unimportant. No other policy variables turned out to be significant.

Siddiqui and his colleagues looked at other ways to indicate how variables move together or do not. For example, to show how weakly related were policy variables and test scores, he compared two hypothetical schools with identical ratings on the variables measuring socio-economic status,

Table 2.5
REGRESSION RESULTS ON HUMANITIES SCORES

	Constant	Income	SES $(Income)^2$	Type of school Boys'	Girls'	Administration Government	Nationalized	Policy variables Salary	$(Salary)^2$	ln number of students	ln percentage of M.Ed.	$\bar{R}^2$	S.E. estimate	F
1. First half of data set (n = 74)	141.70 (1.03)	-37.44 (-1.95)	7.54 (2.24)	-26.30 (-1.77)	31.09 (2.19)	-34.03 (-1.80)	-45.20 (-2.47)	1.03 (2.00)	-0.0008 (-1.67)	—	-20.25 (-5.21)	0.665	36.96	15.51
2. Second half of data set (n = 78) (a)	62.31 (0.34)	15.72 (0.58)	1.47 (0.30)	-10.30 (-0.42)	48.00 (2.04)	-37.30 (-1.29)	-12.86 (-0.49)	1.03 (1.53)	-0.0008 (-1.32)	—	-2.89 (-0.66)	0.418	50.39	6.53
(b)	303.8 (4.29)	24.90 (3.17)	—	-10.00 (-0.40)	45.29 (1.93)	-27.20 (-0.94)	-6.50 (-0.25)	0.16 (2.04)	—	-8.60 (-0.92)	-2.00 (-0.48)	0.418	50.40	7.14

Note: Figures in parentheses are *t*-statistics. Underlining indicates (one-sided) significance beyond the $\alpha = 0.05$ level. One apparent outlier was omitted in calculations on the first half of the data set.

sexual composition, and type of administration. He then supposed that one of the schools had exactly the city-wide average on all policy variables: average teachers' salary, student-teacher ratio, percentage of Masters' level teachers, and so forth. The other school was assumed to have superior ratings on all these variables—at the ninetieth percentile among the city's schools on all of them. Based on regressions that used all the variables and all the observations, the difference between the Science scores predicted for the two schools would be a mere 22.8 points; for Humanities, 7.9 points.

To reinforce the point that SES (income) and policy variables were weakly related in their data, Siddiqui and his colleagues constructed a table of correlations based on the entire data set (Table 2.6).

Returning to the Minister's Problem

Siddiqui and his colleagues wrote up their statistical findings in a technical report. But this did not end their responsibility; in fact, the greatest challenge lay ahead. What did their work have to say about the Minister's policy problem? How much of an increase in examination scores would ensue if one or another of the educational inputs they had studied were increased? What should the Minister conclude (and not

Table 2.6
SES (INCOME) AND POLICY VARIABLES ARE WEAKLY
CORRELATED
(N = 163)

Variables' name	Correlation with SES (income)
Girls' school	0.03
Boys' school	−0.18
Government school	−0.36
Nationalized school	−0.05
Student/teacher ratio	−0.14
Percentage of teachers with first division degrees in B.Ed. (theory)	0.28
Percentage of teachers with first division degrees in B.Ed. (practical)	0.29
Percentage of teachers with M.Ed. degrees	−0.12
Average salary	0.20

conclude) from the results P. F. Siddiqui and his co-researchers had obtained?

*   *   *

Before going any further in the case, the reader should consider how he or she would answer these questions. Teachers may wish to give the case up to this point as an assignment, having students write memoranda to the Minister explaining the policy implications of Siddiqui's work. The following is one of several possible analyses.

The first task is to interpret the regression coefficients derived in Siddiqui's study. Social class is important; the policy variables measured in the study are not. Notice that in the second half of the Science data set, teachers' average salary is no longer significantly related to a school's average science score. In the Humanities data set, the teachers' salary is statistically significant but, for policy purposes, the regression coefficient is too small to make much of a difference. At first blush, then, it appears that Siddiqui should simply tell the Minister, 'none of the policy variables we measured make much difference to examination results'.

But before considering this conclusion in more detail, let us remind the Minister of the shortcomings of this study—and remind ourselves of the perils in interpreting regression-based policy research.

Shortcomings of This Study

Siddiqui's research is limited in several ways. First, the data set is small, cross-sectional, and aggregated. Ideally, one would like to look at all of the city's schools over many years, and one would like student-level information about both academic achievement and socio-economic status, among other variables (policymakers in developing countries are, however, rarely so lucky). Notice, too, that only one city's schools are examined here. The provincial Minister should be reminded that the results may not hold for other places.

Second, the variables available in this study were limited in number and quality. There were no direct measures for innate ability, class-room level inputs, student effort, and so forth. Also, the proxy variables for socio-economic background—itself a murky concept—were crude. And although the dependent variable of examination scores was the one used by most policymakers, one may have doubts about the validity of the standard essay questions that were actually used in the Matric Exams. Most questions seemed to measure memory more than understanding or skill, and the exams may have been subject to cheating.

These are the kinds of difficulties one usually encounters in policy research. This is not an exceptional case. It is important to get in the habit of examining the validity of the dependent variable being used to measure performance and outcome. It is always worth asking whether the model is correctly specified, in terms of what Siddiqui's exploratory approach emphasizes (functional form and choice of variables) and the broader question of the full range of possible variables that might have been included but were not.

Problems with Regression Studies

After considering these methodological limitations, we should move to the policymaker's problems. The Minister's question might be put this way: 'How much of an increase in examination scores would ensue if we increased the provision of one or another of the educational inputs you have measured?'

It is tempting to use the regression coefficients as the answer. The coefficients seem to gauge the expected change in each independent variable, with the often cited but often misunderstood proviso 'other things being equal'. Unfortunately, this is a dangerous translation of what we have learned, and policy researchers must appreciate some of the pitfalls of application.

We *can* assert that—in this sample and with these measures of achievement, socio-economic background, and school variables—no strong associations exist between variations in school variables and variations in achievement. Furthermore, since the exploratory techniques gave school variables many chances to show significantly non-zero effects, we can be rather confident of this negative finding. And by testing our regression on the second half of the data set, we avoided at least one possible spurious conclusion that may have affected the choice of policies. The trick, however, is to connect these results with the Minister's question.

This, of course, enters into the general question of the applicability of regression-based studies. Regression-based evaluations must work with the current educational system as it now stands, rather than assessing what might happen if the *system* were changed. This sometimes overlooked distinction is important for several reasons. Secondary schools in Siddiqui's sample display limited variability in educational inputs, as Table 2.1 makes clear. The data therefore do not allow us to infer what would happen if large changes took place—for example, in the quality of teacher training or in the size of teachers' salaries. Similarly, one can make no inference about the relative effects of various policy variables if the present curriculum were overhauled, the examination system radically changed, or the socio-economic composition of schools greatly altered.

More generally, many people believe that at best regression-based studies like this one, only help us to estimate associations among variables at a given point in time. The Minister's question goes beyond association. He wishes to know what will happen to achievement if certain variables are deliberately changed. If policies are changed to interfere with the educational system the regression itself may be changed; and we may find that the effect of that change could not have been predicted by regressions based on the policies of the past. Practical experience in the analysis of public policies in the United States does not lead one to be confident of predictions based on regressions when the system is subsequently the subject of a policy shift. This is not a fine point of academic nicety, but a fundamental conceptual and practical shortcoming in the analysis of nonexperimental data.[10]

Finally, there are other potential problems with interpreting regressions of this kind. First, it may be dangerous to assume common objective functions and production functions across schools; if these functions differ, the resulting equation may easily be misinterpreted. Second, school policies may already have been differentially set in ways that would bias the coefficients towards zero. For example, if policies are chosen depending on the achievement or achievement potential of the school's students, simultaneous equations may be needed to assess directly the relative contributions of variations in different policies. (In this case, however, my knowledge of the school system in question leads me to accept the idea of uniform objective functions and production functions and to reject the usefulness of simultaneous equations in this context.)

What Do We Tell the Minister?

These caveats are chastening. But they need not reduce us to impotence. What might we say to the Minister? There are some rather uncontroversial conclusions we can draw.

The Minister would probably be interested to know that schools in wealthier areas do not have much smaller classes or much better trained teachers than schools in poorer parts of the city. Contrary to many people's expectations, the study found no strong relationships between SES (income) or SES (region) and school policy variables. This finding may suggest, but does not firmly establish, that in the current school system children from poor homes do worse, regardless of existing variations in school quality.

Our results lend little support to many of the policy prescriptions the Minister regularly receives: 'more teachers, better educated teachers, higher teacher salaries . . . '. Given the present educational system, there is little reason to believe from this study that modest changes along these lines will result in increases in student achievement. The Minister might also be interested to know that these findings are consistent with studies in other developing countries.[11]

One aspect of schools was important: their sexual composition. Girls' schools did better than boys' schools on both tests, even after adjusting for the other variables. It is interesting to ask people to interpret this finding, and the results are often amusing. For my part, I prefer not to assume unequally distributed ability across the sexes. Instead, I emphasize differential enrollment and drop-out rates. The facts for this city are unclear, but nationwide in Pakistan in the mid-seventies, only forty-six girls enrolled in grade one for every one hundred boys; only 41 per cent of girls enrolled finished grade five, compared to 54 per cent of the boys enrolled. In 1973, only 29,000 girls were enrolled in grade ten, compared to 141,000 boys. Although these Pakistan-wide figures overestimate the sexual bias in urban areas, it is still true that more boys than girls undertake Intermediate education.

If enrollments and drop-outs are somewhat correlated with ability, then one might expect the average girl in school to be more able than the average boy, even given equal distribution of ability across the sexes. This correlation does not need to be perfect or even strong, but if some such process is in place, it may explain the differences observed in school achievement. In short, girls may not be smarter than boys, but girls in school may on average be smarter than boys in school.

It may also be worth noting that in studies in the United States, frequently at the high-school level girls do earn better grades than boys.

We may also wish to point out to the Minister the differences between exempted (private), nationalized, and government schools. Exempted schools did better, even after adjusting for socio-economic and other variables. The estimates of the average difference ranged between six and forty-five points, but these differences were not statistically significant in tests using the second half of the data set. They may, therefore, be the results of random effects in the sample.

We would certainly point out what he might have expected we, as analysts, would say: 'We need more research'. For example, the study found that SES (income) was the most powerful predictor of test scores. But this variable is a proxy, and it may mask a host of different effects. Some of these may be amenable to policy interventions and some may not. We cannot yet say, for example, whether more learning goes on outside schools in rich homes, whether richer students are smarter or better nourished or socialized to believe that education is more important, or whether parental income itself has an enabling effect on learning. We can recommend that further study be undertaken with finer SES measures, individual-level data, and a number of years of information. We may wish to advise the Minister to experiment. Unfortunately, the Minister is under pressure to act, but on the other hand he has no strong reason to believe that increases in one input are better than in another, at least not on the basis of this study. We may believe that more fundamental changes in the curriculum, the testing system, and the levels of educational inputs might be productive. But we are not sure. A series of experiments within different secondary schools may yield some answers, as well as satisfying the need to do something politically. No doubt other political and administrative pressures will have to be overcome to do an experiment; they may even be paralyzing. But it might be worth emphasizing that to answer the Minister's question with some confidence, experimentation is the best step we can recommend.

NOTES

[1] Some useful work has been done in other developing countries. A helpful summary is found in John Simmons and Leigh Alexander, 'Factors which Promote School Achievement in Developing Countries: A Review of the Research', in Simmons *et al., The Education Dilemma: Policy Issues for Developing Countries in the 1980's*, Pergamon Press, London, 1979.

[2] Luecke and McGinn criticize applications of regression analysis to educational policy on the grounds that '. . . the complexity of the interactions prevented regression or multiple correlation analysis from reliably estimating the relations built into the simulation model'. (Daniel Luecke and Noel F. McGinn, 'Regression Analyses and Education Production Functions: Can They Be Trusted?' *Harvard Educational Review*, Vol. 45, No. 3, 1975, p. 347.) The applications they dislike are simple linear models posited before examining the data.

[3] 'In this paper I have compared several criteria on the basis of which we can select one regression equation among many candidates . . . (A)ll of the criteria considered are based on a somewhat arbitrary assumption which cannot be fully justified and . . . by slightly varying the loss function and the decision strategy one can indefinitely go on inventing new criteria. This is what one would expect, for there is no simple solution to a complex problem.' (Takeshi Amemiya, 'Selection of Regressors', Tech. Rep. 225, Institute for Mathematical Studies in the Social Sciences, Stanford University, 1976, p. 33.)

[4] Henri Theil, *Principles of Econometrics*, John Wiley and Sons, New York, 1971, p. 605.

[5] See, for example, John W. Tukey, *Exploratory Data Analysis*, Addison-Wesley, Reading, Mass., 1977; Frederick Mosteller and John W. Tukey, 'Data Analysis, Including Statistics', in G. Lindzey and E. Aronson, eds., *Revised Handbook of Social Psychology*, Addison-Wesley, Reading, Mass., 1968; and R. Gnanadesikan, *Methods for Statistical Data Analysis of Multivariate Observations*, John Wiley and Sons, New York, 1977.

[6] Siddiqui may have been encouraged by Barnard's remark: 'The simple idea of splitting a sample into two and then developing the hypothesis on the basis of one part and testing it on the remainder may perhaps be said to be one of the most seriously neglected ideas in statistics, if we measure the degree of neglect by the ratio of the number of cases where a method would give help to the number of cases where it is actually used.' (G. A. Barnard, 'Discussion of Professor Stone's Paper', *Journal of the Royal Statistical Society*, (B), Vol. 36, No. 2, 1974.)

[7] The following formula from Shaycoft was used:

$$r_{\bar{a}\bar{a}} = 1 - \frac{1 - r_{aa}}{n} \left(\frac{s_a^2}{s_{\bar{a}}^2} \right),$$

where $r_{\bar{a}\bar{a}}$ is the reliability of the group mean, r_{aa} is the reliability of individual scores (from a small study involving randomly selected test grades by several randomly selected graders, r_{aa} was estimated to be 0.7), s_a^2 is the variance of individual scores (which we estimated from two large random samples), and $s_{\bar{a}}^2$ is the variance of group means. (Marion Shaycoft, 'The Statistical Characteristics of School Means', in John C. Flanagan *et al.*, *Studies of the American High School*, Co-operative Research Project 276, Project Talent, University of Pittsburgh, 1962.)

[8] Both SES variables are ordinal in character: we believe that category five is greater than category four, four greater than three, and so on, but we do not know how much greater. Conventionally, a linear weighting (that is, category 5 = 5, category 4 = 4, and so on) or dummy variables (if one wishes not to weight at all, but to treat the variables as different categories) are used. However, it may be that the unknown true 'weights' are markedly nonlinear, in which case the conventional alternatives may perform poorly.

[9] The linear two-four system works as follows; array the n categories symmetrically and evenly spaced around zero. Multiply the lowest and highest categories by 4, and multiply the second-lowest and second-highest by 2. Leave the others as they are. For example, in the case of n = 7, the linear two-four weighting would be −12, −4, 0, 1, 4, 12:

Take seven categories	1	2	3	4	5	6	7
Array about zero	−3	−2	−1	0	1	2	3
Multiply	−12	−4	−1	0	1	4	12

For n = 5, the weighting would be −8, −2, 0, 2, 8. (Robert P. Abelson and John W. Tukey, 'Efficient Conversion of Non-Metric Information into Metric Information', in Edward R. Tufte, ed., *The Quantitative Analysis of Social Problems*, Addison-Wesley, Reading, Mass., 1970.)

[10] More generally, see Frederick Mosteller and John W. Tukey, *Data Analysis and Regression*, Addison-Wesley, 1977, chapters 12 and 13; and J. P. Gilbert, Frederick Mosteller, and John W. Tukey, 'Steady Social Progress Requires Quantitative Evaluation To Be Searching', in C. C. Abt, ed., *The Evaluation of Social Programmes*, Sage Publications, 1977.

[11] Simmons and Alexander, op. cit.

CHAPTER 3

DO SCHOOLS CARE ABOUT EQUALITY?

This short chapter focuses on measures of the spread of a distribution, such as the standard deviation. It compares the results of
simulations based on theoretical distributions to observed data.
The chapter also employs multiple regression analysis and
chi-square tests to assess contingency tables.

Studies of cognitive achievement in public schools frequently
focus on average levels of performance, as in the previous
chapter's question, 'what school variables affect a school's
average science score significantly, other things being equal?'
However, investigators in the developed countries are
beginning to look also at achievement *within* schools. Do
some schools consistently have more equality of scores than
others? Do certain school variables significantly affect the
spread of a score within schools, other factors held constant?

These questions about the quality of achievement within
schools are important for educational policy. Schools, like
countries, may care not only about the per capita level of
'goods' produced, but also about the distribution of those
goods. For example, a school may try to have as many
students as possible pass the Matric Exams, even if this
approach means that fast learners may suffer. There may be a
trade-off between raising average scores and narrowing
variability.

Jencks has noted that intra-school inequality is important
in American schools:

> The range of variation for school means is less than half the range
> for individuals. In some ways this is the most important and most
> neglected single finding of the EEOS. It means that if our objective
> is to equalize the outcomes of schooling, efforts to reduce differences
> *between* schools cannot possibly take us very far.[1]

Klitgaard found evidence in the United States that (1) social
background factors do not explain intra-school standard
deviations very well, in contrast to such factors' well-known

This chapter was written by Robert Klitgaard, Sadequa Dadabhoy and Simin
Litkouhi. It originally appeared as 'Cognitive Equality and Educational Policies: An
Example from Pakistan', in *The Pakistan Development Review*, Vol. XVIII, No.1.

DATA ANALYSIS FOR DEVELOPMENT

explanatory power for school means; and (2) year after year and for different tests, some schools consistently have 'tighter' distributions than chance or their socio-economic compositions would predict.[2] Klitgaard speculates that such schools may be consciously aiming at more equality among their students. Brown and Saks found that school variables were significantly related to the spread of scores within schools.[3]

To our knowledge, large-scale studies of cognitive equality within schools have not been carried out in developing countries. In this chapter we examine data from Karachi's secondary schools in the mid-seventies, the same data analysed in the previous chapter. We find that intra-school inequality is large, that our variables for socio-economic background and school policy do not explain variations in intra-school equality across schools, and that a school that is particularly equal on one test is not particularly equal on the other.

Expected Behaviour of the Standard Deviation Statistic

The sample standard deviation is the positive square root of the sample variance (s^2) which is defined as:

$$s^2 = \frac{\Sigma\,(X_i - \bar{X})^2}{n-1}$$

In random samples from a normal distribution, the sample variance is distributed as a multiple of a chi-square distribution with n-1 degrees of freedom. If the sample size n is small (say, n = 10), the chi-square distribution is positively skewed; but by n = 20, the distribution is close to Gaussian.[4] The sample standard deviation will be less skewed. We also expect the variability of the sample variance to be greater for smaller n. Thus schools with smaller number of students tested would have a higher proportion of high and especially low standard deviations, even if their students' scores were drawn from the same distribution as larger schools'.

Assuming normality, the 95 per cent confidence interval on the variance σ^2 is given by the formula:

$$\frac{(n-1)s^2}{\chi^2_{.025}} < \sigma^2 < \frac{(n-1)s^2}{\chi^2_{.975}}$$

Departures from normality in the underlying distribution can greatly affect the accuracy of point and interval estimates of the variance.[5]

Secondary Schools in Karachi

A sample of 207 of Karachi's 348 secondary schools was drawn, stratified by eight socio-economic categories. Data were collected on each school's Matric Exams results for grade ten in both Humanities and Science in 1975-6, and means and standard deviations were computed for each school. Of this sample, 142 schools gave examinations to at least five students in each subject area and had information available on other variables. These additional variables included the socio-economic composition of each school and a variety of school policy variables, as discussed in the previous chapter.

Issues for Analysis

Is intra-school variation large, compared to the variation in examination scores across all schools? The Examination Board does not calculate the Karachi-wide average or standard deviation for students scores. (The standard deviations of school means in our sample were: Science, 73.6; Humanities, 69.9.) We drew two random samples of 1,000 student scores from the schools in our study, one sample for the Science test and one sample for the Humanities. We computed the mean, standard deviation, and skewness of each sample (Table 3.1).

Table 3.1
ESTIMATES OF INTERSTUDENT MEANS,
STANDARD DEVIATION, AND SKEWNESS

Test	Mean	Standard deviation	Skewness
Science	429.8	126.5	−0.14
Humanities	385.6	102.8	0.15

Note: For large samples from a normal population, the standard error of the standard deviation is $\sigma/\sqrt{2n}$; for n = 1,000, about 0.022σ. Thus, 95 per cent confidence intervals for the standard deviation are: Science, 120.9 to 132.0; Humanities, 98.3 to 107.3.

We compared these results with the distributions of scores within schools. Figure 3.1 and 3.2 give histograms of schools' standard deviations on the two tests. Much of the variability in standard deviations among schools can be attributed to

Figure 3.1
HISTOGRAM OF SCIENCE STANDARD DEVIATIONS
(n = 170)

Standard deviation	Number of schools	
50	4	****
60	8	********
70	12	************
80	18	******************
90	36	************************************
100	31	*******************************
110	26	**************************
120	16	****************
130	12	************
140	5	*****
150	2	**

Average = 97.00; Standard deviation = 21.23

Figure 3.2
HISTOGRAM OF HUMANITIES STANDARD DEVIATIONS
(n = 165)

Standard deviation	Number of schools	
20	1	*
30	0	
40	4	****
50	9	*********
60	21	*********************
70	33	*********************************
80	41	***
90	29	*****************************
100	12	************
110	8	********
120	4	****
130	1	*
140	1	*
150	1	*

Average = 79.28; Standard deviation = 19.69

sampling error. Figure 3.3 shows how standard deviations
have less variability for schools with larger numbers of
students tested, as one would expect if, in fact, all students
were samples from a single normal population. To illustrate
this point further, 167 random samples of different sizes
roughly corresponding to the actual distribution of the
number of students tested in Science were drawn from a
normal distribution with μ = 429.77 and σ = 126.48. The
plot of sample standard deviations against sample size had the
same pattern as Figure 3.3, except the samples had on
average larger standard deviations than the actual schools
did, and the standard deviation of the sample standard
deviations in the simulation was 20.65, compared to 21.23
for the actual schools.

The average standard deviation within schools for Science
was 97.7. This is 77 per cent as large as the estimated
standard deviation for *all* Karachi students taking the test.

Figure 3.3
PLOT OF SCHOOL STANDARD DEVIATIONS VERSES NUMBER TESTED, SCIENCE

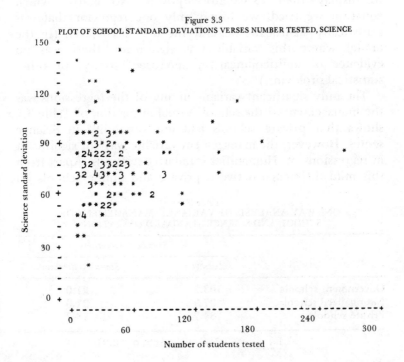

For Humanities, the situation was almost identical: the average standard deviation within schools was again 77 per cent of the interstudent standard deviation.

Intra-school inequality is therefore relatively large. This finding surprised us: we anticipated that most inequality would be between schools. But as Jencks notes for America, the problem of cognitive inequality is to a large extent within schools, not just between them.

Do school policy variables or aggregate socio-economic variables explain differences among schools in their standard deviations? Our variables did not. We performed extensive multiple regression analyses with Science and Humanities standard deviations as the dependent variables, using the techniques of exploratory data analysis discussed in the previous chapters. We experimented with various combinations of regressors, transformations, and interaction terms, paying particular attention to residual plots in looking for useful models. In effect, we gave these variables every chance to display their explanatory power. No matter which equation we tried, we found only one regressor that was statistically significant beyond the $\alpha = 0.10$ level. (In the model where this variable was significant, there was no evidence of multicollinearity, heteroscedasticity, or other statistical problems.)

The only significant variable in any of the regressions was the management of the school. Visual inspection of Table 3.2 shows that private schools had less variability in Science scores. However, the management variable was not significant in regressions on Humanities standard deviations. Apart from this mild difference between private and public schools on

Table 3.2
ONE-WAY ANALYSIS OF VARIANCE: MANAGEMENT OF
SCHOOL AND SCIENCE STANDARD DEVIATIONS

	Standard deviations	
	Average	Standard deviation
Government schools	103.2	21.0
Nationalized schools	97.9	21.0
Private schools	84.7	18.2

$F_{2,162} = 6.27$, significant at $\alpha = 0.01$

Science tests, we find no support for the idea that our variables for school policies or socio-economic background are consistently and importantly effective in equalizing (or widening) scores within schools.

Do certain schools consistently have more (or less) equality among their students' scores? If a school is effective in pursuing equality (or in widening scores), we might expect that its standard deviations for the two different tests would tend to be smaller (larger) than those of other schools. We might anticipate a positive correlation between schools' standard deviations on the two tests.

In these data, however, no such phenomenon was observed. Figure 3.4 depicts the situation. The correlation between the standard deviations was only 0.02, statistically insignificant; the rank correlation was 0.00. (In contrast, the correlation of school average scores on the two tests was 0.78.)

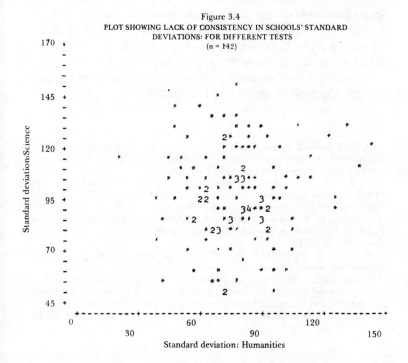

Figure 3.4
PLOT SHOWING LACK OF CONSISTENCY IN SCHOOLS' STANDARD
DEVIATIONS: FOR DIFFERENT TESTS
(n = 142)

Conclusions

A surprisingly large amount of the cognitive inequality among all secondary students in Karachi was within schools, not between them. To equalize average scores across schools would therefore not mitigate most of the disparities observed in student learning. In itself, this finding has important implications for educational policy. If one cares about cognitive equality, one cannot simply focus on raising the quality of the poorest schools.

But if inequality within schools is important, do school policies affect it? Our evidence is consistent with, but does not prove conclusively, a negative answer—in the particular context of Karachi's secondary schools in 1975. Not only do none of our variables for socio-economic background or school policies explain variations in intra-school equality, but no school seems more (or less) likely to provide equality across different tests. A number of explanations may be offered for these results. We hypothesize that either secondary schools in Karachi do not care much about the equality of learning among their students or they do not currently have effective means for narrowing (or widening) differences in achievement among students. Future research, particularly with longitudinal data and more precise measures, will be required to verify our conjectures.

NOTES

[1] Christopher S. Jencks, 'The Coleman Report and the Conventional Wisdom', in Frederick Mosteller and Daniel P. Moynihan, eds., *On Equality of Educational Opportunity*, Vintage, New York, 1972, p. 86.

[2] Robert E. Klitgaard, *Achievement Scores and Educational Objectives*, The Rand Corporation, Santa Monica, Calif., 1974; also 'Going Beyond the Mean in Educational Evaluation', *Public Policy*, Vol. 23, No. 3, Winter 1975, pp. 59-79.

[3] Byron W. Brown and Daniel H. Saks, 'The Production and Distribution of Cognitive Skills Within Schools', Journal of Political Economy, Vol. 83, No. 3, June 1975, pp. 571-93.

[4] K. A. Brownlee, *Statistical Theory and Methodology in Science and Engineering*, second edition, Wiley, New York, 1962, p. 199.

[5] For research on estimating spread in non-normal distributions, see Robert C. Blattberg and Nicholas J. Gonedes, 'Estimaters of the Parameters of the Student Distribution and Other Fat-Tailed Distributions', Report 7501, Centre for Mathematical Studies in Business and Economics, University of Chicago, January 1975.

CHAPTER 4

INFLATION IN UNIVERSITY GRADES

This chapter illustrates the use of statistical tools to describe phenomena as well as to test hypotheses. Histograms over time clearly portray the inflation of university grades. Regression analysis enables several hypotheses about that inflation to be rejected.

In the mid-seventies the University of Karachi suffered from rampant inflation in marks. Work of the same relative and absolute quality earned a higher score in 1975 than it did two years before. To put it another way, 50 marks were not worth as much as they used to be. The average score given in one humanities course was 66, but two years earlier it was 49. Several years earlier a score above 80 was almost unknown. In 1975, one course in the Economics Department had an *average* score of 83.

Figures 4.1 and 4.2 show histograms of average grades over time in a sample of Karachi University courses. The teachers surveyed said that on average students were not learning more than before. Like the rupee and the pound, University grades had suffered serious inflation. What might be the reasons for this phenomenon?

The Function of Grades

Grades or marks are supposed to signify how well students have mastered a particular subject. At Karachi University, both grades and marks are given. Grades range from A to F, marks from 100 to zero. In most subjects, it used to be that 60 marks or above meant an A. If a student's average in all courses was above 60, he or she would receive a first-class degree. In one year, teachers tried to define a score of 70 marks as the lowest A and 60 as the cut-off for B grades. But students protested vehemently, and an average of 60 marks or above still earned a first-class degree.

This chapter was written by Robert Klitgaard. Azizeh Currimbhoy provided research assistance. Sayeed Shaikh, Nighat Moin, and Tahira Qureshi helped to collect the data.

Figure 4.1
THE DISTRIBUTION OF AVERAGE ARTS MARKS OVER TIME

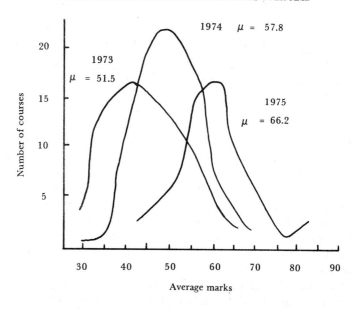

Figure 4.2
THE DISTRIBUTION OF AVERAGE SCIENCE MARKS OVER TIME

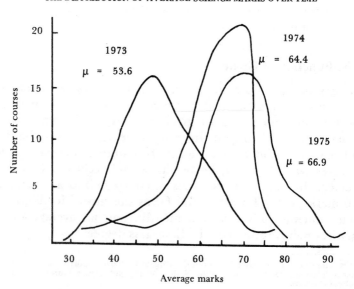

Grades have two related functions. First, they provide an *incentive* for students. Students try hard—perhaps too hard—to get good grades. We say 'too hard', because since grades are not perfectly correlated with student learning, students may neglect learning skills that are not or cannot be tested or graded. Students may also try to achieve high grades through methods that do not aid learning, such as cheating or memorizing. Our small surveys at the University of Karachi indicated that on average over half the students cheated on examinations.

Grades also function as a *credential*. If employers believe that marks correlate with ability or with the amount of useful learning attained by students, employers may use marks in hiring decisions. Many publicly advertised job descriptions in Pakistan carry a requirement such as 'second-class degree in mathematics or science' or 'first-class M.A. in economics'. The young graduate bears credentials: not only his or her degree type and subject area, but also first, second, or third-class standing.

Grades determine first, second, or third-class degrees, which in turn affect the probability of being employed. A study[1] of 2,800 Karachi University graduates of the class of 1971 shows that, three and a half years later, only 9.8 per cent of those in the labour force were unemployed. This figure is much lower than is commonly believed. But only 6.6 per cent of those with first-class degrees were unemployed, compared to 9.2 per cent of second-divisioners and 12.1 per cent of those with third-class degrees. It is also likely that a first-class degree entitles one to a *better* job, on average.

Who Benefits from Inflated Grades?

Because of the decision to continue defining first-class as 60 marks and above, there will be more first-class degrees than in the past. Who gains from this inflated number of first-divisioners? Clearly, those who otherwise would have received a lower-class degree are better off. But those who would have been first-class even with a cut-off of 70 marks are worse off, because there will be more first-divisioners with whom to compete for jobs and overseas training.

Graduates of previous years are also worse off. They may be likened to investors whose currency has suddenly been devalued. Their first or second-class degrees are no longer worth as much, because more of those currencies are in circulation.

Employers are also worse off. As proxies for ability and attainment, the credentials 'first-class' or 'second-class' are no longer as informative. First-class students now have a wider variance, weakening the information value of the signal. Unless new proxies can be devised, we expect labour markets to work even less efficiently than they did before.

One other group probably loses: the teachers. Let us assume that teachers desire that students learn and that grades are one powerful incentive to induce learning. Then the inflation of grades leaves teachers as a whole with a less potent set of rewards. Many students may learn less, because they can more easily attain the credentials they desire.

Why Does Inflation Occur?

Let us consider in more detail the ways that teachers and students are affected by inflation in grades. We believe that inflated grades can be partially explained in terms of incentives introduced by the abandonment of outside examinations.

The semester system was introduced at Karachi University in 1973. One significant change associated with the semester system concerned the grading of examinations. Before, students were given tests that were designed by outside examiners. The grading was also done by outsiders. The teacher's role was simply to teach a prescribed curriculum. The evaluation function belonged to others.[2]

Under the semester system, teachers design and grade their own tests. Teaching and evaluating functions are merged.

Students care about their grades. They know that their teachers determine the grades and may badger them for higher grades, which is not pleasant for the teachers. Consider the following simple model. Each individual teacher has an incentive to give his students slightly higher grades than his colleagues give, so that his students will not badger him. Certainly, no teacher wishes to give lower grades than his colleagues. In effect, teachers have incentives to compete with their colleagues: the higher the grades one gives compared to other teachers, the less one is subjected to student hostility.

Therefore, we hypothesize the following cause for the inflation of grades. Under the semester system *each individual teacher finds it in his own interest to give slightly higher grades, even though when all teachers do this all teachers are worse off.* As a result, each year teachers find that the average grade given goes up.[3]

Other Possible Explanations

Among the other possible causes of inflated grades are changes in the teachers and students that occurred from 1973 to 1975. The University of Karachi's enrollment expanded greatly. The average class size increased. If larger classes are associated with higher grades, then any 'demographic' change might explain at least part of the inflation.

Similarly, the composition of teachers changed: there were more lecturers. About 28 per cent of the teachers in our 1974-5 sample were lecturers compared to about 18 per cent in 1972-3 If lecturers are easier graders, their increased numbers may explain increases in average grades.

Empirical Analysis

We investigated these latter and several other hypotheses, using data from a sample of fourteen to eighteen departments in the Faculty of Science and fourteen to eighteen departments in the Faculty of Arts and Islamic Studies. (The number depended on the year examined.) Data were laboriously collected on each of the final-year courses in these departments, for the years 1972-3, 1973-4, and 1974-5. (More recent figures had not been compiled in the departments.) For each course and year, the average and the standard deviation of marks were computed. In addition, information was collected on the following variables: number of students receiving marks; rank of teacher (professor, associate professor, assistant professor, and lecturer); teacher's degree (doctorate or master's); and teacher's age, years of teaching experience, and sex.

For the purposes of analysis, the data were divided into six sets: 1972-3 Arts, 1972-3 Science; 1973-4 Arts, 1973-4 Science; 1974-5 Arts, and 1974-5 Science. We report here the results of six separate multiple regression analyses using the average marks in the course as the dependent variables. We attempted to answer several questions. Do any of our variables consistently explain variations in average marks, other things being equal? In particular, do larger classes have significantly higher averages? Do lecturers give higher marks?

Using these data, we cannot test directly our favoured hypothesis—the one based on teachers' incentives. But we can test some of the alternative explanations. If none of the variables consistently and significantly affect average grades, we may perhaps advance our preferred hypothesis with greater assurance.

Our regression strategy was exploratory. We had no *a priori* model that specified the exact functional form to be used. Therefore, we experimented with different combinations and transformations of the regressor variables. We studied residual plots for evidence of curvilinearity, outliers, heteroscedasticity, or clustering. Our intention was not to overlook any significant variables should they exist; our exploratory approach probably led to an upward bias in the regression coefficients we obtained.[4]

Table 4.1 displays the pattern of significant variables with their signs from regression equations for each of the six data sets. The pattern of significant variables showed no changes when apparently superfluous variables were dropped, although sometimes the significant ones become more significant. Thus, we believe Table 4.1 is a fair representation of the pattern of the results.

As it turns out, this pattern is all we need to dismiss the idea that larger class sizes, or more lecturers, lead to higher average grades. The coefficient on number of students is significantly *negative* in five of the six equations: larger classes get lower marks, not higher ones. The effect of being a lecturer can be gauged by examining the coefficients of the other three possible ranks of teachers (professor, associate professor, and assistant professor). In the 1972-3 Arts equation, all the others have significantly positive coefficients, meaning that lecturers gave *lower* grades on average. In the other five equations, we cannot reject the hypothesis that lecturers give the same grades as other teachers.

The coefficients on the sex dummy are inconsistent. In three of the six equations, male teachers give higher grades, other things being equal; but in Science 1974-5, female teachers give higher grades. The percentage of women teachers had increased only slightly over time (9 per cent in our 1974-5 sample compared to 5 per cent in 1972-3); therefore, we reject the idea that this factor explains the University's inflation in grades.

Table 4.1
SIGNIFICANT VARIABLES AND THEIR SIGNS

Variable	Arts 1972-3	Science 1972-3	Arts 1973-4	Science 1973-4	Arts 1974-5	Science 1974-5
Number of students	_**	_**	_**	n.s.	_**	_**
Professor	+**	_*	n.s.	n.s.	n.s.	n.s.
Associate professor	+**	n.s.	n.s.	n.s.	n.s.	n.s.
Assistant professor	+**	n.s.	n.s.	n.s.	n.s.	n.s.
Age	n.s.	n.s.	+*	n.s.	n.s.	n.s.
Experience	_**	n.s.	_*	n.s.	n.s.	n.s.
Degree	_**	n.s.	n.s.	n.s.	n.s.	+*
Sex	+**	n.s.	+**	n.s.	+**	_**
Number of courses	77	72	85	86	61	72
$\bar{R}^2$	0.31	0.07	0.11	0.02	0.21	0.14
F	**	n.s.	n.s.	n.s.	**	**

Note: Significance of regression coefficients was assessed using two-sided *t*-tests. * = significant at the $\alpha = 0.10$ level; ** = significant at the $\alpha = 0.05$ level; n.s. = not significant. Dummy variables were used for professor, associate professor, assistant professor, degree (1 = doctorate, 0 = master's), and sex (1 = male).

What Can Be Done About Inflation?

Although the topic goes beyond our statistical work, we would like to conclude by considering several possible cures for grade inflation.

Grade on a Curve. Grading on a curve means that in each course a specified number of students will receive a specified score. For example, 7 per cent of the students in each course will receive A's, 16 per cent B's, 50 per cent C's, and so forth. (By the way, we found no evidence of grading on a curve at the University of Karachi.)[5]

The curve certainly stops inflation. But at a cost: the curve's rigidity. Only so many A's can be given, regardless of whether the subject is nuclear physics (with self-selected superior students) or basket-weaving (presumably having slower students).

Ranks. Suppose that a teacher simply ranked his students instead of giving marks. A '1' would mean the student was the best in the course, a '10' tenth best in the course, and so forth. Provided that ties were not allowed, 'grading by ranks' would stop inflation.[6]

Ranks have disadvantages. Being number ten in a large, difficult course may signify a brilliant scholar, but may be a dubious honour in a small, easy course. Ranks are sensitive to the number of students in a course. In a small class a pupil may be number fifteen but be at the bottom. In a large class, number fifteen may be in the top 10 per cent. One remedy for this problem would be to give students a percentile grade—for example, marking a student at the ninety-second percentile would mean that 92 per cent of the class were below him or her on performance. Still, being number ten or at the eighty-fifth percentile may signify a brilliant student in a difficult course but be a dubious honour in a very easy course.

External Graders. A third cure for the inflation of grades is to go back to the old system and separate the teaching and evaluative functions. External examinations would be of help. There may be pedagogical disadvantages, though. The old system was accused of freezing the curriculum year after year and limiting the teacher's creativity in the class-room.

Departmental Guidelines.   Each department would set forth a rough curve to be followed. The curve would not be rigid, but indicative. For example:

A	5 to 20 per cent of students
B	15 to 40 per cent of students
C	25 to 60 per cent of students
D	10 to 45 per cent of students
E	5 to 25 per cent of students.

Teacher's grades would be examined in a department meeting each semester, before the grades were finalized. If a teacher were close to either of the extremes in each category (for example, to 5 or 20 per cent in the A category), he or she would have to explain why. Rarely, might a teacher be allowed to exceed the guidelines, upon demonstration of a good reason.

The Deans would approve each department's guidelines. Some sort of standardization across departments would be desirable. Such procedures would probably have led to a revision of the grading practices in the Sindhi Department, which during our period of study gave grades that averaged ten or more points higher than any other department.

This proposal would probably eliminate some clear abuses in grading. The guidelines themselves, however, might be subject to erosion. One would expect that teachers would gravitate toward the upper percentage limits of the high grades and the lower percentage limits of the low grades. One might foresee that over time the guidelines themselves would be subject to inflation. Strong leadership by department Chairmen and Deans would help to prevent it.

No grades.   If we abolished grades, there would be no grade inflation. Is this an unrealistic alternative? Perhaps, but we should contemplate critically the shortcomings of the grading system. Consider the prevalence of cheating on tests. Consider the poor quality of faculty grading.[7] Consider the inherent unreliability of any grading system. (The scores we give all too often depend on what we had for breakfast, or on the day's humidity.) Would it not be worthwhile to foresake grading altogether?

This step was attempted with little success in the late sixties at a number of universities in the United States. Students were given either a pass or a fail. After several years, students and faculty members pressed for a new category above pass: 'honours'. After another year, a 'high honours' category was begun. So, at some universities at least, a few years after the 'abolishment' of grades, categories very similar to A, B, C, and F were back in force.[8]

Nonetheless, abolishing grades is a good alternative to keep in mind. Considering extreme steps brings the issues into sharper focus.

Conclusions

The inflation of grades helps some students in the short run, but it is generally harmful in the long run. Inflation can be expected under circumstances when teachers find it possible and in their individual interests to give slightly higher grades (or, at least, no lower grades) than their colleagues. The semester system *per se* is not at fault—rather, it is the combination of internal examinations and poor discipline among faculty members that may explain grade 'inflation'.

Among the cures, the most desirable may be the establishment of departmental guidelines on grading. No step will succeed, however, without a commitment by University teachers to create meaningful and firm standards of competence. Thus, the inflation of grades raises even more fundamental issues, which deserve widespread consideration: how should we measure and reward merit, and what happens in systems where the measures or the rewards go awry?

NOTES

[1] Rabia Raffi, Robert E. Klitgaard, and Eric Gustafson, 'Idle Brains: Graduate Unemployment in Karachi', Applied Economics Research Centre, University of Karachi, mimeograph.

[2] For a description of student strikes and other problems with the introduction of a similar system in Nepal, see Louis Hayes, 'Educational Reform and Student Political Behaviour in Nepal', *Asian Survey*, Vol. XVI, No. 8, August 1976, p. 759ff.

[3] Readers familiar with the theory of games will recognize this situation as an n-person Prisoners' Dilemma. For an interesting presentation of the dynamics of such dilemmas, see George A. Akerlof, 'The Market for "Lemons,": Quality

Uncertainty and the Market Mechanism', *Quarterly Journal of Economics*, Vol. 84, No. 3, August 1970.

4 Henri Theil advises: 'Given the present state of the art, the most sensible procedure is to interpret confidence coefficients and significance limits liberally when confidence intervals and test statistics are computed from the final regression of a regression strategy in the conventional way. That is, a 95 per cent confidence coefficient may actually be an 80 per cent confidence coefficient and a 1 per cent significance level may actually be a 10 per cent level'. *(Principles of Econometrics,* John Wiley and Sons, New York, 1971, pp. 605-6.)

5 For example, we examined the standard deviation of marks given within courses. There was considerable variation in the standard deviations across courses in a given year; no curve was in force. Furthermore, a course that had a large standard deviation one year might have a small one the next. The standard deviations of marks given in the same course over successive years were almost uncorrelated: −0.06 for 1972-3 to 1973-4 (n=76), and 0.04 for 1973-4 to 1974-5 (n=54), neither being significantly different from zero.

6 If ties were allowed, a teacher could inflate his class's grades by giving a large number of '1' or '2' or '3' rankings. Without ties, each course can only have one number '1'.

7 A detailed study of one department uncovered amazing instances of unfair grading. One teacher graded students on the first test only. On subsequent tests, each student received exactly the same score, and on the final exam, the score was simply multiplied by two. One teacher always gave two sisters identical marks.

8 Such experiments may even have stimulated subsequent inflation of grades, as Gerald Grant and David Riesman describe for 'one large private University' in the United States: 'Grades began to inflate in the late 1960s, so that 16 per cent of the class of 1970 graduated with honours, 19 per cent of the 1971 graduates, 23.5 per cent of the 1972 class, and in 1973, 27 per cent. Selectivity reached a peak in 1965, and declined slightly as grades rose. Once faculty had sold freedom as a way of placating the pressures we have described, they began to pass out high grades as bait to attract students to departments and courses they were no longer required to attend'. ('An Ecology of Academic Reform', *Daedalus*, Vol. 104, No. 1, Winter 1975, p. 182.)

CHAPTER 5

THE DISTRIBUTION AND
USE OF FERTILIZER IN SIND

Tables of data can be usefully analysed in several ways. This chapter uses the analysis of variance and robust two-way analysis to examine district level usage of fertilizer. Regression analysis is also used to explore the economic value of fertilizer. This chapter emphasizes what can and cannot be learned from already aggregated data.

Introduction

The benefits of efficient fertilizer use in Pakistan are experimentally well-documented.[1] Although in 1975 Sind led Pakistan in fertilizer use—29.6 nutrient-lbs. per acre vs. 22.6 nutrient-lbs. per acre in Punjab[2]—the quantities applied were nowhere near recommended doses.[3] More efficient fertilizer use—that is, *more* of the right *kinds* of fertilizer applied in the right *places* at the right *times*—is widely agreed to be necessary for achieving optimum agricultural output. But how much more, and which kinds? Where and when? Unfortunately, little micro-level analysis of fertilizer use on farms in Sind had been carried out. Further, no systematic look at the process of distributing fertilizer in the province had ever been taken.

An ideal study of fertilizer distribution and use would have three parts. First, it would employ technical, economic and social information to determine the optimal pattern of fertilizer use. This pattern would be determined by equating marginal social benefits with marginal social costs, where benefits and costs would include considerations of equity as well as efficiency. The second step would be an evaluation of farmers' demand and possible policies for equating demand and optimal use, such as increased provision of extension and credit services. Thirdly, there would be an analysis of possible administrative methods for implementing the needed policies.

This chapter was written by Michael Wallace, with assistance from Robert Klitgaard.

This chapter represents a preliminary step towards the ideal study. Recognizing that fertilizer policy decisions must be made in the absence of precise information, we begin in a spirit of exploration: *our aim is to see what we can (and cannot) learn from district-level data, which comprised the only information available.* What useful conclusions can be reached with incomplete and imprecise information? Using such data, can we find the most fruitful areas for further, more detailed study?

Sales and Stocks[4]

Data on irrigated areas for five major crops (wheat, rice, cotton, sugar-cane, and maize),[5] total fertilizer sales, and fertilizer sales per irrigated acre were tabulated for Sind on a district-wise basis. (Karachi was omitted due to its extremely low cultivated acreage and fertilizer use; Badin, a new district, was incorporated into the districts of which it formerly was a part.)

The district-wise variation in fertilizer sales per irrigated acre was significant. For example, Tharparker used seven times as much fertilizer per acre as Jacobabad. This variation—as measured by the standard deviations of districts' average fertilizer use—had not decreased during the period 1969-70 to 1974-5.

Detailed records of Sind Agricultural Supplies Organisation (SASO) sales and stocks positions were not centrally available, so a precise analysis of inventory positions was not possible. (Esso stock information was not available; however, Esso is selling all its production.) As an initial step the SASO sales/stock ratios for each district for the period July 1974 to June 1975 were analysed (Table 5.1).

Several observations may be made:

- The sales/stocks ratios were surprisingly low. This was prima facie evidence of poor inventory management and distribution. However, imports in 1974-5 totalled 62,439 nutrient-tons, and sales were 33,216 nutrient-tons; thus current sales were 53 per cent of current imports.
- Different districts had significantly different ratios. For

Table 5.1
SASO NITROGENOUS* FERTILIZER SALES/STOCKS RATIOS, JULY 1974 TO JUNE 1975

	Jul	Aug	Sep	Oct	Nov	Dec	Jan	Feb	Mar	Apr	May	Jun	1974-5 (average)
Khairpur	.04	.04	.01	.01	.02	.06	.16	.00	.01	.00	.03	.02	.04
Jacobabad	.06	.04	.20	.04	.01	.00	.08	.00	.00	.01	.06	.07	.05
Sukkur	.02	.02	.04	.00	.00	.01	.13	.04	.04	.00	.02	.02	.03
Nawabshah	.10	.02	.02	.02	.10	.07	.11	.00	.01	.04	.07	.01	.05
Larkana	.29	.45	.40	.06	.02	.12	.37	.00	.02	.01	.12	.41	.21
Sanghar	.09	.03	.02	.07	.09	.08	.14	.01	.01	.07	.08	.01	.06
Tharparkar	.10	.05	.04	.11	.10	.03	.17	.00	.01	.09	.03	.03	.06
Dadu	.08	.17	.17	.05	.07	.24	.41	.07	.03	.01	.05	.10	.15
Hyderabad	.01	.01	.01	.01	.03	.02	.11	.00	.00	.02	.02	.01	.02
Thatta	.07	.06	.05	.03	.01	.01	.14	.01	.02	.03	.03	.05	.04
Total	.07	.05	.05	.04	.06	.05	.15	.01	.01	.04	.04	.03	.05

Analysis of variance:　Row $F_{(9,99)} = 7.55$　Column $F_{(11,99)} = 5.05$

* SASO phosphatic fertilizer sales/stocks ratios were also analysed. The results followed the same general pattern as the nitrogenous ratios and are presented in A. H. Kadri, M. Wallace, and A. Hai, *Fertilizer Distribution and Use in Sind*, Research Report No.4, Applied Economics Research Centre, University of Karachi, November 1976.

example, Larkana's average sales/stocks ratio was ten times Hyderabad's average ratio.

• Different months had significantly different ratios. For example, January's sales/stocks ratio over all districts was fifteen times February's ratio.

What explains these observations? Several possibilities exist:

• *Low sales/stocks ratios* may reflect poor record-keeping.
• *District differences* may be due to variations in record accuracy, salesmanship, or stock policies. Also, fertilizer may not always be used in the district where it is purchased.
• *Monthly differences* may arise if receipts of imported fertilizer do not coincide with farmers' demand, or if optimal use varies from month to month.

Visits to the sales outlet would be necessary to verify the accuracy of these explanations. The analysis of aggregated data of the kind we have examined is only the first step. It can guide our subsequent investigations, but additional research is needed to provide detailed answers.

A 'Value of Production' Function

Where are the benefits of additional fertilizer greater? Differences in marginal value products (the marginal value of the additional output resulting from increasing fertilizer use by one unit) for fertilizer would provide the first indication of possible adjustments to make in fertilizer distribution. The ideal calculation of these values would utilize farm-level, time-series data on inputs use, and yields for various crops. Inputs measured would include land, labour, seed, water, fertilizer, mechanical power, and pesticides. From this information, production functions would be estimated for each crop for each district of Sind. Prices of inputs and outputs would be used to calculate optimum input and output levels. A study of the relationship between the fertilizer distribution system and actual fertilizer use would link fertilizer distribution and crop output. Policy recommendations for improving fertilizer distribution would follow.

Unfortunately, many of these data were not available. Farm-level information was not available. Crop-wise data on the use of labour, seed, water, fertilizer, mechanical power, and pesticides are not available. This study has been restricted to analysing *district-level* data on land, fertilizer, and irrigated acreage. Crop-wise acreage and production data were available on a district basis, but the lack of corresponding data on fertilizer and water usage eliminated the possibility of estimating production and cost functions for each crop.

What can be learned from the existing data? We expect that rational farmers will allocate fertilizer across crops in order to maximize profits: thus, to begin, a 'value of production function' was estimated:

$$V/A = f (N/A, P/A, I/A)$$

where V = value (Rs 000) of the production of the five major crops (wheat, rice, cotton, sugar-cane, and maize), N = nitrogeneous fertilizer sales (nutrient-tons); P = phosphatic fertilizer sales (nutrient-tons); I = irrigated acreage for the five crops (000); and A = total acreage for the five crops (000). Value was calculated using district-wide 1969-70 prices.

Ordinary least squares regression analysis (OLS) was used to estimate this function, using data for six years (1969-70 to 1974-5) and ten districts. The means and standard deviations of these variables were:

Variable	(V/A)	(N/A)	(P/A)	(I/A)
Mean	396.78	16.54	2.40	0.98
Standard deviation	176.70	10.09	2.17	0.02

The (I/A) variable exhibits very little variation; almost all the acreage of these crops was irrigated. Actual quantities of water applied would be a much better variable to include in the regression analysis.

Data were not available on some inputs that probably affected output and that were also likely to be positively correlated with fertilizer use. For example, there was no information concerning the use of improved seeds and pesticides, nor the actual quantities of water applied. We thus expect that the regression coefficients of the fertilizer variables in our equation will be positively biased. The true coefficients should be closer to zero than the ones we will estimate.

Aggregated data have another problem. The process of aggregation eliminates variations in rates of fertilizer application within districts, which may affect fertilizer productivity. For example, if two districts have the same average rate of fertilizer application, but one district spreads fertilizer evenly over all its acreage and the other concentrates its use on particular areas or crops, we would expect the districts to have different yields: aggregated data using averages only, miss this possibility.

We estimated the 'value of production function' using both linear and logarithmic specifications. The logarithmic form is more appealing since inputs are to some extent complementary and marginal products are probably not constant. A visual examination of the residual plot for the linear specification also revealed possible heteroscedasticity (non-constant variance of the errors). There was no such evidence with the logarithmic form.

The results of the logarithmic specification are presented below (t-statistics are given in parentheses below each estimated coefficient):

$$\ln (V/A) = 6.48 - 0.22 \ln (N/A) - 0.04 \ln (P/A) + 0.39 \ln (I/A)$$
$$(29.17)(-2.26) \qquad (-0.54) \qquad\qquad (0.21)$$

$\bar{R}^2 = 0.24$, S.E. estimate = 0.35, $F_{(3,56)} = 7.08$, n = 60

These results are astounding: fertilizer seems to have negative productivity. The coefficients for both ln (N/A) and ln (P/A) are negative; in the case of ln (N/A), the negative sign is statistically significant. But we expected the coefficients of the two fertilizer variables to be positive. The findings are even more surprising when we recall that these coefficients are biased upwards because of the omitted variables. How might we explain these anomalous findings?

We began by examining the variation among districts. We looked at scatterplots of the standardized residuals from the regression. These plots revealed district-wise clustering but revealed no definite yearly trends.

From these plots we learned that *districts are different.* If we want to estimate fertilizer productivity, we must statistically control for district. Otherwise, the effects of districts will be confused with the effects of fertilizer.

How much do districts differ? Are there significant year-to-year variations that may be masking the true effects of fertilizer? To find out, we carried out an analysis of variance on V/N ratios, that is output value per unit of nitrogenous fertilizer, analysed by district and by year.[6] The analysis is presented in Table 5.2.

Analysis of variance (ANOVA) is a technique for testing whether differences between group averages are significantly different from zero. In our problem, we want to know whether the differences we observed between the average V/N ratios of different districts and different years could be explained by chance. We are asking the question, 'If each district (or each year) really had the same average V/N ratio, what is the probability that by chance alone we would observe the differences in V/N ratios that actually occurred?'

Define the following notation:

$$r \; = \; \text{number of districts (rows)} \; = 10$$
$$c \; = \; \text{number of years (columns)} \; = 6$$
$$x_{ij} \; = \; \text{V/N ratio for district } i \text{ in year } j$$

$$\bar{\bar{x}} = \sum_{i=1}^{10} \sum_{j=1}^{6} x_{ij}/60 = \text{grand mean}$$

$$\bar{x}_i = \sum_{j=1}^{6} x_{ij}/6 = \text{district } i \text{ mean}$$

$$\bar{x} = \sum_{i=1}^{10} x_{ij}/10 = \text{year } j \text{ mean}$$

Row i effect $= \bar{x}_i - \bar{\bar{x}}$
Column j effect $= \bar{x}_j - \bar{\bar{x}}$
ijth entry in ANOVA table $= x_{ij} - \bar{x}_i - \bar{x}_j - \bar{\bar{x}}$

A positive (negative) row effect means that a district has an above-average (below-average) V/N ratio. A similar statement holds for column effects, which refer to years rather

Table 5.2
TWO-WAY ANALYSIS OF VARIANCE OF V/N RATIOS

	1969-70	1970-1	1971-2	1972-3	1973-4	1974-5	Row effect	Rank
Khairpur	−17.24	−5.62	5.86	4.52	7.56	4.94	−35.68	6
Jacobabad	−25.68	8.90	5.07	−7.10	−2.84	21.65	123.45	1
Sukkur	−27.89	13.60	3.59	5.51	6.24	−1.01	−3.58	4
Nawabshah	−22.61	−8.38	5.23	11.94	5.74	8.07	−40.57	8
Larkana	22.78	0.89	−12.45	−9.07	17.48	−19.59	16.25	3
Sanghar	−25.57	−9.33	8.82	12.13	7.10	6.87	−42.97	10
Tharparkar	−22.36	−8.13	8.79	11.04	4.93	5.74	−41.52	9
Dadu	−24.29	−3.06	6.03	7.02	5.33	9.01	−24.29	5
Hyderabad	−21.83	−13.78	−0.08	13.63	6.89	15.21	−38.75	7
Thatta	104.70	25.00	−30.84	−49.61	−58.37	−50.85	87.66	2
Column effect	24.91	11.16	−7.08	−12.17	−7.77	−9.04	52.31	
							Grand mean	

Row F $(9,45)$ = 20.70   Column F $(5,45)$ = 2.12

than districts. F-statistics can be computed based on differences among row (or column) averages. If the F-statistic is large enough, we say that the differences observed are statistically significant at some previously specified level, say $p < 0.05$.

Notice how different are the row effects in Table 5.2. There is considerable variation among districts in the value of output per unit of nitrogenous fertilizer input. For example, Jacobabad and Sanghar differ by 166.42, which means that these districts differed by Rs 1,66,420 in the value of their crop output per nutrient-ton of nitrogenous fertilizer.

Is this variability statistically significant? Consider first the fact that:

$$
\underbrace{\sum_{i=1}^{10} \sum_{j=1}^{6} (x_{ij}-\bar{\bar{x}})^2}_{\substack{\text{total sum of} \\ \text{squares} \\ \text{(TSS)}}} = \underbrace{\sum_{i=1}^{10} \sum_{j=1}^{6} (\bar{x}_i-\bar{\bar{x}})^2}_{\substack{\text{row sum of} \\ \text{squares} \\ \text{(RSS)}}}
$$

$$
+ \underbrace{\sum_{i=1}^{10} \sum_{j=1}^{6} (\bar{x}_j-\bar{\bar{x}})^2}_{\substack{\text{column sum of} \\ \text{squares} \\ \text{(CSS)}}} + \underbrace{\sum_{i=1}^{10} \sum_{j=1}^{6} (x_{ij}-\bar{x}-\bar{x}_j+\bar{\bar{x}})^2}_{\substack{\text{error sum of} \\ \text{squares} \\ \text{(ESS)}}}
$$

To test for the equality of V/N ratios among districts, we compute the statistic:

$$
\frac{\text{RSS}/(r-1)}{\text{ESS}/(r-1)(c-1)} = \frac{\sum_{i=1}^{10} \sum_{j=1}^{6} (\bar{x}_i-\bar{\bar{x}})^2 /(10-1)}{\sum_{i=1}^{10} \sum_{j=1}^{6} (x_{ij}-\bar{x}_i-\bar{x}_j+\bar{\bar{x}})^2 /(10-1)(6-1)}
$$

If each district really has the same average V/N ratio, this statistic will follow an F-distribution with 9 and 45 degress of freedom. In the case at hand, the computed F-ratio is 20.70. Checking a table of the F-distribution, the probability that an F-statistic with 9 and 45 degrees of freedom would exceed 20.70 if the districts had the same V/N averages is less than 1 per cent. Thus, we are confident that the differences observed in Table 5.2 are not the results of chance alone.

In the same way, we can test the hypothesis that each year really has the same average V/N ratio. The test statistic is now:

$$\frac{\text{CSS}/(c-1)}{\text{ESS}/(r-1)(c-1)} = \frac{\displaystyle\sum_{i=1}^{10}\sum_{j=1}^{6}(\bar{x}_j-\bar{\bar{x}})^2/(6-1)}{\displaystyle\sum_{i=1}^{10}\sum_{j=1}^{6}(x_{ij}-\bar{x}_i-\bar{x}_j+\bar{\bar{x}})^2/(10-1)(6-1)}$$

If each year really had the same average V/N ratio, this statistic would have an F-distribution with 5 and 45 degrees of freedom. Here the computed F-ratio is 2.12. The probability that an F-ratio with 5 and 45 degrees of freedom exceeds 2.12 is less than 10 per cent. The differences among the districts are more pronounced than the differences among the years.

The analysis of variance is an excellent tool when data are 'well-behaved'. However, Table 5.2 contains outliers, or observations that are quite different from the general pattern. For example, Thatta's V/N ratio for 1969-70 is much higher than any other ratio. These data are not well-behaved. Outliers may contaminate the estimation of row and column effects by ANOVA. To avoid this contamination, one may employ the statistical technique of 'robust two-way analysis'. This method calculates row and column effects using medians instead of means.[7] That is, the grand median is the median of all the V/N ratios (rounded to the nearest integer); the row effects are the medians of the rows after the grand median and the row effects are subtracted from each V/N ratio. There is no statistic similar to the F-ratio to test for significance in the robust analysis of variance. The results of this analysis appear in Table 5.3. It confirms that the differences among districts are greater than the differences among years.

Table 5.3
ROBUST TWO-WAY ANALYSIS OF V/N RATIOS

	1969-70	1970-1	1971-2	1972-3	1973-4	1974-5	Row effect
Khairpur	6	-1	0	-2	2	-1	-7
Jacobabad	-1	16	1	-12	-7	18	150
Sukkur	-4	20	-1	0	1	-6	24
Nawabshah	0	-3	-1	5	0	2	-12
Larkana	51	11	-13	-11	16	21	40
Sanghar	-4	-5	2	4	0	0	-13
Tharparkar	0	-4	2	3	-2	-1	-12
Dadu	-1	2	0	0	-1	3	5
Hyderabad	0	10	-7	6	0	8	-9
Thatta	-225	67	0	0	-27	-20	80
Column effect	3	7	0	-4	-1	-2	22
							Grand median

Is Fertilizer a Good Investment?

Rational farmers will use fertilizer only if the value of the output increase is greater than the cost of the fertilizer. The cost of fertilizer is fixed throughout Pakistan. Thus, the demand for fertilizer should be greater where the increase in the value of the output is greater.

In economic terms, rational farmers should demand more fertilizer in the districts where its marginal value product (MVP) exceeds its marginal cost. Similarly, to maximize the value of output, more fertilizer should be allocated to these same districts.

Calculating marginal value products for districts is not easy. We have only six data points for each district. Regression analysis is of limited use with such a small number of observations. But for what it is worth, four regressions were used to estimate districts' marginal value products:

- OLS estimation of $\ln (V/A) = a + b \ln (N/A)$
- Robust estimation[8] of $\ln (V/A) = a + b \ln (N/A)$
- OLS estimation of $(V/A) = a + b (N/A)$
- Robust estimation of $(V/A) = a + b (N/A)$

These results were consistent in their ranking of districts' marginal value products, as shown in Table 5.4. Jacobabad, Thatta, and Dadu had high positive values; and Khairpur, Larkana, Nawabshah, and Sukkur had negative values. The Friedman rank-correlation test indicates that the probability is less than 0.001 that such consistent rankings are merely random.[9]

Despite the consistency of the ranks of these estimates, we need more accurate estimates of marginal value products. These calculations did not control for water, nor was any account taken of yearly weather variation.

Still, it is alarming that in four districts the results are *negative*. In only thirteen of the forty calculations are the estimated marginal value products of fertilizer greater than Rs 3, the relevant marginal cost. Quite simply, these results are inconsistent with experimental findings, which show that fertilizer use is quite profitable.

Is fertilizer a good investment? A rational farmer would compare the marginal value product of fertilizer with its

Table 5.4
ESTIMATED MARGINAL VALUE PRODUCTS

	Method 1		Method 2		Method 3		Method 4	
District	MVP	District	MVP	District	MVP	District	MVP
Jacobabad	152.30	Jacobabad	143.02	Jacobabad	168.95	Thatta	21.05
Dadu	13.44	Thatta	18.08	Thatta	20.55	Jacobabad	15.39
Thatta	13.11	Dadu	14.98	Tharparkar	3.02	Dadu	14.62
Sanghar	2.33	Tharparkar	4.22	Hyderabad	2.98	Hyderabad	1.06
Hyderabad	2.05	Hyderabad	0.11	Sanghar	2.28	Tharparkar	0.48
Tharparkar	2.03	Sanghar	0.01	Dadu	1.15	Sanghar	0.20
Khairpur	-0.14	Nawabshah	-0.63	Sukkur	-0.16	Khairpur	-1.60
Larkana	-0.57	Khairpur	-0.89	Khairpur	-0.23	Nawabshah	-3.04
Nawabshah	-3.11	Larkana	-1.10	Larkana	-1.52	Larkana	-3.14
Sukkur	-14.34	Sukkur	-9.57	Nawabshah	-3.16	Sukkur	-10.44

Friedman rank-correlation statistic: $\chi_r^2 \, (9) = 32.29$

marginal cost. Since Table 5.4 gives crude estimates of marginal value products, and the marginal cost is approximately Rs 3, fertilizer is not a good investment for farmers—except in Jacobabad, Thatta, and Dadu.

Jacobabad consistently ranks very high in both row effects and MVP calculations. Thatta and Dadu are also high, but less consistently. We believe the fertilizer situation in Jacobabad deserves further investigation. Perhaps lessons in fertilizer use may be learned from what is happening there. Jacobabad may be reaping the benefits associated with the initial use of fertilizer. On the other hand, perhaps artefacts in the data are responsible for Jacobabad's seemingly outstanding performance.

Conclusions

What have we learned, and what should be our next steps in research on fertilizer distribution and use?

This exploratory analysis shows both the problems and the possibilities of working with aggregate and incomplete data. The problems are obvious, but the possibilities are encouraging.

Because we have aggregated data and lack information on important variables, we cannot accurately estimate the marginal productivity of fertilizer on farms in Sind, by crop or by district, and thus we cannot determine the theoretical optimal allocation of fertilizer. However, we have been able to point out districts where the benefits of increased fertilizer use appear greater. This may be the first step in improving fertilizer allocation.

Because we lack data on sales outlets, we cannot effectively evaluate the distribution system. However, we can point to apparent deficiencies in the system: the next step is to study the possibilities for improvement.

On the basis of our exploratory analysis, we have identified fruitful areas for further, more detailed research on fertilizer distribution and use. The following key findings may be highlighted:

- SASO records revealed *astonishingly low sales to stock ratios* for nitrogenous and phosphatic fertilizers. It seems important to examine this finding in detail. Were the large inventories warranted? Or were they fictitious? To find out, field visits to a selected sample of sales outlets is advisable.

- *The estimated returns to fertilizer use were generally negative.* This finding, based on a series of analyses of aggregated data, demands confirmation from farm-level studies. The next step would be to collect and analyse farm-level data, including information on water use, agricultural inputs, and quality of land.

- *District-to-district variations in-fertilizer use and productivity are surprisingly large.* Average fertilizer use in Tharparkar was seven times that in Jacobabad. Estimates of fertilizer productivity in Jacobabad are positive, and very high; estimates for Khairpur, Larkana, Nawabshah, and Sukkur are negative. A small but intensive study of the fertilizer situation in Jacobabad may provide valuable information regarding fertilizer use and productivity.

The potential agricultural output of the Indus Valley has been estimated to be more than three times the current actual output. Experimental results indicate that increased fertilizer distribution could result in large social gains and improved distribution and use in greater agricultural output.

We believe there is little point in going any further with secondary data that are overly aggregated and incomplete. But notice how even these data can be of help in identifying where more detailed, disaggregated studies should take place. We have identified some promising areas of inquiry. Some would involve field studies; some would entail careful econometric analysis of farm-level data. Success in investigating any of these areas will require the interest and co-operation of policymakers, farmers, fertilizer distributors, and analysts. As more is learned, credit agents, extension personnel, and agronomists are likely to become involved. All have important roles to play in the important task of finding better ways to distribute fertilizer for optimal agricultural production. So do statisticians and economists.

NOTES

[1] A. S. Khan, *Derivation of Fertilizer Crop Response and Optimum Levels of Fertilization for Various Crops/Areas*, University of Agriculture, Lyallpur, 1975.

[2] US AID, *Project Paper: Pakistan—Agricultural Inputs Loan*, Islamabad, 1975.

[3] A. S. Khan, op. cit.

[4] The data in this section were obtained from the Bureau of Statistics, Planning and Development Department, Government of Sind, Karachi; and from Sind Agricultural Supplies Organization, Karachi.

[5] It is estimated that more than 90 per cent of the nitrogenous and more than 80 per cent of the phosphatic fertilizers are used on these crops. See Sind Agricultural Supplies Organization, 'Action Plan, 1975-6', cyclostyled, Karachi, no date; and Esso Pakistan Fertilizer Company, Ltd., *Fertilizer Consumption and Market Development in West Pakistan*, Karachi, 1971.

[6] We also carried out analysis of variance on the standardized residuals of the regression equation. These results are presented in A. H. Kadri, M. Wallace, and A. Hai, *Fertilizer Distribution and Use in Sind*, Research Report No. 4, Applied Economics Research Centre, University of Karachi, November 1976.

[7] John W. Tukey, *Exploratory Data Analysis*, Addison-Wesley, Reading, Mass., 1977.

[8] Tukey, op. cit. Robust estimation consists of summarizing high and low groups of observations in data sets and fitting lines based on these summary points.

[9] On this test, see Frederick Mosteller and Robert E.K. Rourke, *Sturdy Statistics: Nonparametrics and Order Statistics*, Addison-Wesley, Reading, Mass., 1973, chapter 13.

CHAPTER 6

THE ECONOMICS OF TEACHER TRAINING

This chapter presents a detailed exploratory data analysis. Two common problems are dealt with: the treatment of nonresponses and the construction of multiple regression models in the absence of an *a priori* model. Chi-square tests are used to analyse variables taken two at a time. The benefits of looking at plots of residuals are also illustrated. Finally, the results of the statistical analyses are connected to policy choices regarding teacher education.

I. INTRODUCTION

Pakistan's shortage of teachers is said to be severe, especially in rural areas. Yet little is known about the supply of new teachers. What are the costs of teacher training? What has been the employment experience of newly trained teachers? How many have jobs, what are the salaries, and what is the length of job search? How many teachers would be willing to consider rural employment? What demographic, personal, and educational characteristics affect these aspects of teacher employment? These question are addressed in this study of Karachi's experience in the mid-seventies.

The research reported here, and in our longer monograph on the subject,[1] also has methodological and pedagogical interest as an example of exploratory data analysis. Readers interested solely in the policy questions may skip directly to section IV; those interested primarily in the statistical issues should concentrate on section II (procedures) and III (data and analysis).

II. NOTES ON STATISTICAL PROCEDURES

This section constitutes an informal justification for the statistical methods employed in analysing the teacher training data. Its objectives are: (1) to outline the 'philosophy' behind

Robert Klitgaard was assisted by Muneer A. Khan, Mohammad Arshad, Naheed Niaz, and Khalil Y. Siddiqui, in this chapter which has appeared in a less comprehensive form in *Comparitive Education Review*, Vol. 29, No. 1.

the exploratory techniques utilized in the study; (2) to comment on how to interpret the results from regression equations chosen through exploratory data analysis; and (3) to outline the differences between ordinary least squares regression and logit analysis, in the case of a binary dependent variable.

An Exploratory Philosophy

We may search for hypotheses, or we may try to confirm hypotheses already held. The second disposition has dominated much of statistics and econometrics. Models are posited, often on the basis of a theory; and statistical tests are carried out, based on assumptions about underlying frequency distributions.

In many cases, we have neither a well-specified model nor a rationale for distributional assumptions. Although it is easy and conventional simply to assume a certain model (e.g., linear additive) and a certain multivariate distribution (e.g., normal), there is often no convincing reason for doing so. Even when a microeconomic model is appropriate as the basis for statistical work, real life almost always introduces complications; for example, the errors stemming from missing data and proxy variables. And of course microeconomic theory itself is replete with assumptions, as its most distinguished practitioners freely advertise.

Thus in many real-life settings, we lack a convincing model or a hypothesis. We must search rather than confirm. In these situations a different 'philosophy' of data analysis is useful. Following John Tukey, we may call this philosophy 'exploratory data analysis'.

> The processes of criminal justice are clearly divided between the search for the evidence—in Anglo-Saxon lands the responsibility of the police and other investigative forces— and the evaluation of the evidence's strength—a matter for judges and juries. In data analysis a similar distinction is helpful. Exploratory data analysis is detective in character . . . Unless the detective finds the clues, judge or jury has nothing to consider . . . *Exploratory data analysis can never be the whole story, but nothing else can serve as the foundation stone—as the first step.* [2]

We will use statistical tools to try to uncover 'what the data seem to be saying'.

An example may be useful. Often in statistical and econometric studies, the analyst employs linear regression analysis. The ordinary least squares technique (OLS) may assume, in the simple case of one dependent variable Y and one independent variable X, a particular specification:

$$Y_i = b_o + b_1 X_i + e_i$$

where b_o and b_1 are constants. The error term e_i is assumed to fulfill these assumptions:

$$E(e_i) = 0$$
$$E(e_i e_j) = 0 \text{ if } i \neq j$$
$$= \sigma^2 \text{ if } i = j$$

where σ^2 is a constant.

There may well be departures from these assumptions in real life. The specification of the model may be incorrect. Perhaps an additional independent variable should be included. The variables may need re-expression; for example, perhaps X should be transformed to logarithms. We may need to discriminate among the individual observations: we may weight certain observations less, or we may remove wildly deviant observations from the analysis.

If the OLS assumptions are met, then well-known statistical tests can be used to confirm or reject prior hypotheses. But if those assumptions cannot be supported, then there is no guarantee that the theoretically optimal statistical tests actually test anything in the real world. The computed regression coefficients and confidence intervals are similarly cast into limbo.

In our case of teacher training, we are worried about several matters. First, we do not have an *a priori* model of how our variables concerning teachers' demographic, educational, and personal characteristics affect various dimensions of teachers' employment experience (unemployment, salary, months of job search, willingness to take a rural job). We do not even know which variables we should include in our model. We do not know the proper functional form of the regression equation.

Second, we have differing numbers of nonresponses on the different variables. A teacher who reported her wage may not have answered the question about her intermediate division; another teacher may have answered all the questions except the one about mother tongue. We cannot conveniently assign a value to the missing answer. Nor can we eliminate all teachers who failed to answer any question, for we would have a drastic reduction in sample size.[3]

As a result of these problems, we have adopted a variety of exploratory techniques. We examine variables in pairs, looking for clues about which variables are most important and which may require transformations. We fit simple regressions and then examine plots and tables of residuals *vis-a-vis* a string of other variables, with the nonresponses included. We try a number of complicated multiple regressions, paying particular attention to residuals and to the stability of regression coefficients. We report a variety of results, not just one, so that the reader can draw some of his or her own conclusions about what the data reveal.

The Interpretation of Exploratory Regression Results

With the approach we have adopted, our resulting regression equations cannot be interpreted in the strict sense of 'confirmatory' data analysis. When the inclusion or exclusion of variables in the nth regression is based on the statistical significance of variables in the n-1th regression, the sampling distribution of estimators in the nth regression is affected. In particular, the t-statistics and F-statistics cannot be used in exact tests of hypotheses about the regression coefficients or the regression equation as a whole.

If we knew exactly how the estimators were affected by adopting a particular 'regression strategy', we could make allowances. For example, we might hope that the bias of coefficients and of t-tests could be analysed *given* a certain multi-stage selection procedure for the included variables. Then adjusted tests could be used.

Researchers have tried to do this. Unfortunately for practical work, estimates of bias depend on the unknown true values of the coefficients, as well as on the distribution of underlying error terms. The data analyst is left in limbo.[4]

One solution is to test the final equation we choose on another set of data, as we saw in chapter 2. With large data sets, one may set aside half the observations and choose a preferred equation using the other half, later testing that result on the first half. In the case at hand, we did not have enough observations to afford this luxury.[5]

We must, therefore, be cautious in interpreting the coefficients and summary statistics of our regressions. They may be biased upwards: we are likely to have a higher $\bar{R}^2$, for example, than our model 'really' deserves.[6]

OLS Explorations with a Binary Dependent Variable

When we are trying to predict whether a recently trained teacher has a job or not, or whether he or she would consider a rural job or not, the variable of interest is binary. Such dichotomous variables can cause statistical problems, especially in the context of regression studies like ours.

For example, consider the simple function:

$$R_i = \alpha_o + \alpha_1 A_i + E_i,$$

where R = would consider a rural job (1 = yes, 0 = no), and A is age. We estimate α_o and α_1 using the data at hand. It is possible that the sum $\alpha_o + \alpha_1 A_i$ might take values greater than 1 or less than 0, depending on A_i. R_i, on the other hand, must equal 0 to 1. Therefore, E_i given A_i can only take two values: $-(\alpha_o + \alpha_1 A_i)$ and $1-(\alpha_o + \alpha_1 A_i)$. Now according to OLS assumptions, $E(E_i) = 0$ for any A_i. Therefore,

$$p\left(E_i = (\alpha_o + \alpha_1 A_i)\right) = 1-(\alpha_o + \alpha_1 A_i) \text{ and}$$
$$p\left(E_i = -(\alpha_o + \alpha_1 A_i)\right) = \alpha_o + \alpha_1 A_i.$$

But since $\alpha_o + \alpha_1 A_i$ may be negative or greater than one, but a probability cannot, the OLS specification has a serious problem.

Researchers have shown that OLS estimators in such cases are inefficient and, if the independent variables are dummy variables, inconsistent.[7] Some scholars have, therefore, recommended the use of 'logit', 'probit', and other specifications, instead of OLS.

These other specifications, however, are not without their own shortcomings. Some are statistical. It is true that the logit specification is relatively simple, symmetrical, convenient in handling grouped data, and mathematically attractive because under certain assumptions a maximum likelihood estimator can be derived.[8] But these mathematical reasons are unrelated to the issue of the appropriateness of the logit specification for the data at hand. Furthermore, the maximum likelihood estimates may not exist in certain cases.[9]

Other shortcomings are computational. Computer programmes for logit analysis did not exist in Pakistan when we carried out this research. In general, logit programmes take much more time to run than OLS programmes, and therefore the many runs necessitated by our exploratory techniques would have been extremely costly.

We can, however, adopt a strategy like the one used in this chapter. We use OLS and other techniques to select a set of independent variables, on the assumption that t-tests for OLS regression coefficients are roughly accurate indicators of what MLS would show. If one assumes multivariate normality and equal covariance matrices among the independent variables, the OLS approach provides exact t-tests concerning the independent variable.[10] In our applications, which contained dummy independent variables, one cannot assume multivariate normality. Some research, however, has shown that the OLS-based estimates of the logit parameters agree closely with the MLE estimates, even with dummies as independent variables.[11]

III. DATA AND ANALYSIS

Programmes for teacher training vary greatly in Pakistan. Brief refresher courses for experienced teachers have become more widespread. Such courses usually last less than a year and sometimes only a few weeks. They may try to teach the teachers new technical or vocational skills (for example, in agriculture), or they may attempt to recharge the teacher's battery of basic subjects (such as, reading and arithmetic).

Traditional degree programmes, on the other hand, put both fresh graduates and experienced teachers through at least one year's training that results in a formal degree and impart the basic skills of the profession. Several programmes exist. The 'highest' degree is the Master of Education (M.Ed.); the 'lowest' is the Primary School Teachers' Certificate (P.T.C.). Falling somewhere in between are the degrees of Bachelor of Education (B.Ed.) and Certificate of Teaching (C.T.). The Drawing Teacher's Certificate (D.T.C.) and Oriental Teacher's Certificate (O.T.C.) refer to those specific skills.[12] In this chapter, we focus on B.Ed., P.T.C., and C.T. programmes.

The Costs of Teacher Training

How much does it cost to train a teacher? Surprisingly few data are publicly available. 'Development costs' and 'recurring costs' are often distinguished, although the line between them is hard to draw. The Planning Commission's working papers for the 1975-80 plan estimated 'recurring expenditure per trainee per annum' at Rs 200. Was this accurate for Karachi's teacher training programmes?

We collected detailed cost and environmental information for six of Karachi's colleges and institutes that trained teachers. This arduous exercise and its results are detailed in our monograph. Space permits only a few major findings:

- Recurring costs per student varied by a factor of six. We could not attribute much of these variations to different accounting rules. The average recurring cost across all colleges was more than double the Planning Commission's projection.
- Costs were lower in colleges with more rapid expansion. The rank correlation between growth in enrollment from 1970 to 1975 and growth in average per pupil operating costs over the same period was −0.77. Real costs had declined over that period. Officials told us that the quality of training had also gone down, as

enrollments were increasing by 10 to 60 per cent per year.

- Students paid only a small part of the costs of their training. The proportion varied greatly, but a rough average figure would be a fifth or less of the total recurring expenditure per student.

The Sample Survey

We surveyed June 1974 graduates from Karachi's four largest teacher training colleges. We excluded experienced teachers and looked only at those classified as 'fresh' graduates by the colleges. After enumerating the graduates via a careful examination of each college's records, we drew a stratified random sample of 400 graduates, representing 55 per cent of B.Ed. graduates. We designed a questionnaire and pretested it on a small, independent random sample of the graduates. The pretesting convinced us to change some questions and to delete others, including questions about parents' income and education.

Revised questionnaires were sent by registered mail to the stratified sample in June 1975, thirteen months after our respondents had graduated. Follow-up letters were sent to non-respondents in August. By September about 240 responses had been returned. We randomly selected thirty-two of the non-respondents and interviewed them personally. All of them were available and willing to respond; many said that they had posted their answers despite our not having received anything. Non-respondents did not significantly differ from respondents in salaries or months to first job, so we have some confidence that our sample is 'representative'.[13]

Nonetheless, not all respondents answered every question. As a consequence, our data analysis strategy was hampered by incomplete information on our respondents—a common problem in research using sample surveys.

Before we get to the data analysis, consider first some basic facts about the respondents. Table 6.1 gives a summary, and there are many surprises. Perhaps the most astounding result is the *unemployment rate* of 55.7 per cent. *Despite the 'shortage' of teachers, over half of our sample were jobless*

Table 6.1
SOME BASIC INFORMATION ON NEWLY TRAINED TEACHERS

Variable	Response rate (percentage)	Statistics
Age	100	Average 23.2 years; standard deviation 3.7
Sex	99	Men 13 per cent; Women 87 per cent
Married	99	Yes 14 per cent; No 86 per cent
Religion	100	All were Muslims
Native tongue	95	Urdu 91 per cent; Punjabi 3 per cent; Bengali 3 per cent; Sindhi 2 per cent; Pushto 1 per cent; English less than 1 per cent;
Matric division	99	I 17 per cent; II 49 per cent; III 32 per cent; Pass 1 per cent
Inter division	73	I 2 per cent; II 53 per cent; III 43 per cent; Pass 2 per cent
Graduate division	52	I 2 per cent; II 67 per cent; III 31 per cent; Pass 0 per cent
Degree type	100	B.Ed. 47 per cent; M.Ed. less than 1 per cent; C.T. 22 per cent; P.T.C. 31 per cent
Held job before teacher training	98	Yes 25 per cent; No 75 per cent
More study soon[1]	99	Yes 85 per cent; No 15 per cent
Employment status	97	Employed as teacher 40 per cent Employed in other job 3 per cent Unemployed 55 per cent In school 2 per cent
Rate of labour force participation[2]	94	95.3 per cent
Unemployment rate[3]	94	55.7 per cent
Seeking work[4]	n.a.	Yes 77 per cent; No 23 per cent
Would work in rural areas	70	Yes 31 per cent; No 69 per cent

[1] The question was: 'Do you plan to study more in the near future?'
[2] Non-participants include those now in college and those who are both unemployed and not seeking work.
[3] Defined as (number unemployed and seeking)/number in labour force.
[4] Includes respondents who were already employed.

thirteen months after graduating from teacher training college.
(Of those who had jobs, 7 per cent were not employed as
teachers.) As we shall see later, the job openings were in rural
Pakistan, not in urban areas like Karachi. In short, we observed a problem of structural unemployment.

How many in our sample would be *willing to work in rural
areas?* The answer was somewhat discouraging: only 31 per
cent of those responding to the question said they would.
Fully 30 per cent of the subjects who returned questionnaires
did not answer this question. This is a higher rate of non-response than for almost any other question, and we suspect
that many of those who did not respond meant to say 'no'.

Nonetheless, our respondents say that they *want to work.*
Fully 93.2 per cent are classified as participating in the
labour force. Of the unemployed, 94 per cent are seeking
work. Remarkably, of those already holding jobs, 51 per
cent responded affirmatively that they were now seeking
work.

As noted above, our sample included only students
classified as 'fresh' by the teacher training colleges, a term
which refers not to personality but to teaching experience.
Nonetheless, fully 25 per cent of our 'fresh' respondents said
they held a *teaching job before entering a teacher training
college.* Only 43 per cent hold a job *after* finishing teacher
training college. The enhancement of employability does not
seem to be monumental.

A final surprising result concerns the percentage who say
they plan to study more in the near future: 85 per cent. Our
graduates do not believe they have finished their formal
education, even in the short run.

These surprising facts piqued our curiosity. What attributes of these newly trained teachers were associated with
their chances of being employed? With their salaries if employed? With the number of months it took to get a job?
With their willingness to work in rural areas?

Employment

We have no *a priori* model that tells us which combination of
attributes predicts whether a newly trained teacher will be

employed or not. We may suspect that teachers who did better in college will be more likely to be employed, that men will be more likely to have jobs than women, and so forth. But we have no theory that specifies how these and other attributes interact in a situation like ours.

We therefore adopt an exploratory approach. Our first step is to look at two-way tables, which may give us hints about differences and causes within our sample.

To demonstrate our general procedure, consider the relationship between unemployment and sex. Let us construct a two-by-two table between unemployment and sex (Table 6.2). For convenience, we only consider the 252 respondents who were not in college and who responded to questions about employment status, age, and sex. Only 30.3 per cent of the males were unemployed compared to 60.2 per cent of the females. Thus, sex seems importantly related to the probability of getting a job.

Might this result be a fluke, a result of sampling error? We can never be sure. But we can assess the probability that a difference as large as the one we observed could have occurred if, in fact, the true probabilities of being unemployed were the same for men and women.

Suppose the probability of being unemployed was the same for men and women. Assuming that sex and employment status were statistically independent, our best guess of this probability is the actual percentage unemployed, or $142/252 = 56.3$ per cent. Since there are thirty-three males, we would expect that $33 \times 142/252 = 18.6$ or nineteen males would be unemployed, instead of the ten unemployed males actually observed. We can create a table of expected counts under the assumption of independence in a similar fashion (Table 6.3).

Table 6.2
UNEMPLOYMENT AND SEX

	Male	Female	Total
Unemployed	10	132	142
Employed	23	87	110
	33	219	252

We may now compute the chi-square statistic χ^2. Let O_{ij} be the observed value for row i and column j in Table 6.2, and E_{ij} be the expected values in Table 6.3. Then:

$$\chi^2 = \sum_{i,j} \frac{(O_{ij} - E_{ij})^2}{E_{ij}}$$

is distributed as chi-square distribution with one degree of freedom. For a two-by-two table, the Yates continuity correction 'is easy to use and often improves the agreement between the distribution of χ^2 and its asymptotic χ^2 distribution under the null hypothesis'.[14] The revised statistic for a two-by-two table is

$$\chi^2_{2\times2} = \sum_{i,j} \frac{(O_{ij} - E_{ij} - 1/2)^2}{E_{ij}}$$

For the case at hand, the computed $\chi_{2\times2}$ is 9.30. Checking a table of chi-square distribution, the probability that a χ^2 variable with one degree of freedom would exceed 9.30 is less than one per cent. Therefore, with 99 per cent confidence we can reject the hypothesis that recently trained male and female teachers have the same chance of being employed.

We applied the same test to see how a number of other variables, taken one at a time, were related to unemployment. Some of the tests involved two-by-three tables. Table 6.4 summarizes the results. In our monograph, we examined these findings in detail, as clues to the next steps of analysis. Here only one result can be noted: the lack of relationship between a teacher's academic record and being employed. Only the teacher's division in Matric—the results of an exam taken at the end of the tenth grade—was significantly related

Table 6.3
EXPECTED COUNTS IF UNEMPLOYMENT
AND SEX WERE INDEPENDENT

	Male	Female	Total
Unemployed	18.6	123.4	142
Employed	14.4	95.6	110
	33.0	219.0	252

to unemployment at the $p < 0.05$ level ($\chi^2 = 8.53$, 2 d.f.). Most of the chi-square came from first divisioners, the best students, of whom only 37 per cent were unemployed, compared to 58 per cent of the second divisioners and 69 per cent of the third divisioners. No significant differences emerged by later performance at either the Inter or graduate levels. The unemployment rates by degree type were: B.Ed., 56 per cent; C.T., 50.9 per cent; and P.T.C., 61.5 per cent. These differences proved not to be statistically significant at the $p < 0.05$ level.

Only 43 per cent of this group was employed.[15] Figure 6.1 summarizes some interesting facts about the employed teachers. Since 94 per cent were teaching all subjects—rather than only science and mathematics, for example—specialization in a teacher training college may be less functionally important than commonly believed. Also, it is noteworthy that 10 per cent of the employed teachers held an additional job.

Tabular analysis revealed interesting patterns among the employed teachers. Proportionally more women became primary school teachers than men, but there are no statistically significant differences between sexes on type of school (government, nationalized, or exempted) or language of school. Proportionally more women held an additional job; proportionally more men would consider a rural job (62.5 per cent v. 32.2 per cent).

Table 6.4
RESULTS OF CHI-SQUARE TESTS FOR THE INDEPENDENCE
OF UNEMPLOYMENT AND ELEVEN OTHER VARIABLES TAKEN
ONE-BY-ONE

Significant $p < 0.01$	Significant $p < 0.05$	Insignificant $p < 0.05$
Sex; Teaching job before teacher training (yes, no); language (Urdu, non-Urdu); would work in rural areas (yes, no, nonresponse)	Matric division (I, II, III)	Would work in rural areas (yes, no); Inter division (I, II, III); graduate division (I and II, III) Degree type (B.Ed., C.T., P.T.C.); has children (yes, no); lived with parents after graduation (yes, no)

We begin our search for the factors that determine unemployment by noting an important feature of our data set: nonresponses. Many people did not answer every question, and different people left out different answers. We must explore the data, insofar as possible, while leaving in the nonresponses.

As noted above, varying nonresponses on different questions precluded our beginning with several large, preliminary regression equations with all the attributes that we believed had a chance to be significant predictors. If we had eliminated everyone who did not respond to at least one question, our sample size would have been drastically reduced. Our alternative was to begin with a small equation and to look carefully at the residuals plotted against each variable not included in the equation. Our first equation used age and sex as the independent variables.

Equation (1) $U = 0.52 + 0.0065 \text{Age} - 0.28 \text{ sex}$
$\qquad\qquad\qquad$ (2.10)   (0.75) $(-2.82)*$

$\bar{R}^2 = 0.036$, S.E. estimate $= 0.49$, $F = 5.69$,* $n = 252$

Figure 6.1
SOME CHARACTERISTICS OF EMPLOYED TEACHERS

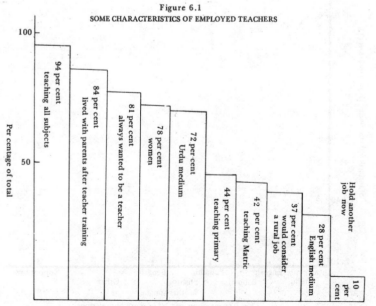

Note: n = 83, but due to differing percentages of nonresponse, each question is based on a different number of respondents.

(In all regression results reported in this chapter, figures in parentheses are *t*-statistics, and the criterion for statistical significance, subject to the caveats raised in Section II, is $\alpha = 0.05$, indicated by an asterisk.) Sex was statistically significant: women were less likely to be employed, age held constant. Age was not significant, sex held constant. The percentage of variation explained ($\bar{R}^2$) was very low (3.6 per cent, adjusted for degrees of freedom).

Even with nonresponses, residuals could be usefully plotted against each of the possible predictors. For example, Figure 6.2 shows the plot of residuals against language spoken in childhood. Notice that we can simply ignore the nonresponses as we look at the plot. Those with mother tongues other than Urdu tended to have positive residuals—that is, they tended more often to be employed. Only 32

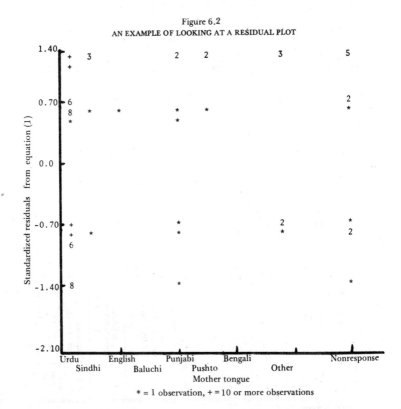

Figure 6.2
AN EXAMPLE OF LOOKING AT A RESIDUAL PLOT

* = 1 observation, + = 10 or more observations

per cent of them were unemployed, well below the percentage for the whole sample. Even after statistically controlling for age and sex, it appears' that mother tongue may be a predictor of employment status. Because of the small number of people with non-Urdu mother tongues (twenty-two) and because no one language's residuals seemed obviously higher, we decided to use language as a zero-one independent variable in the next step of our statistical exploration (0 = Urdu, 1 = non-Urdu).

We examined sixteen residual plots from equation (1), trying to identify candidates for inclusion into the next regression equation. We selected variables whose residual plots seemed to show nonrandom patterns. For example, we found that those with first division Matric certificates were more likely to be employed than second or third divisioners, whereas second and third divisioners looked about the same. Again we created a dummy variable for inclusion in the next regression (0 = II, III, or pass; 1 = I). In addition, we ended up including 'lived with parents after school',[16] type of degree, and 'had teaching job before teacher training college'.[17]

Table 6.5 presents the results of three of the most interesting subsequent regressions. Three variables were statistically significant and had relatively stable regression coefficients regardless of the other variables in the equation: men, those with first-class Matric certificates, and those who had teaching jobs before were more likely to be employed, other things being equal.

Those with mother tongues other than Urdu were more likely to be employed, but the result was not statistically significant at $\alpha = 0.05$. Age, degree type, and lived with parents did not turn out to be statistically significant, once other factors were held constant.

The importance of the variable 'had teaching job before teacher training college' made us worry. Were we truly explaining the unemployment of *fresh* teachers? Would the same results hold if we eliminated from consideration all those who previously held teaching jobs?

To find out, we dropped the previously employed teachers from the sample and painstakingly repeated all our statistical

Table 6.5
REGRESSIONS ON UNEMPLOYMENT

Equation		Constant	Sex	I Matric	Job before teacher training	Urdu	Age	Live with parents	P.T.C.	B.Ed.	$\bar{R}^2$	S.E. estimate	F
						Variable							
1) U	=	0.36 − (0.94)	0.25* (−2.34)*	+ 0.17 (2.05)*	−0.20 + (−2.57)*	0.20 + (1.87)*	0.076 (0.65)	+ 0.012 (0.10)	−0.024 + (−1.31)	+ 0.15 (1.62)	0.096	0.47	3.95*
2) U	=	0.62 − (4.50)*	0.29* (−2.83)*	+ 0.17 (2.00)*	−0.22 + (−2.92)*	0.029 (1.28)			−0.024 + (−1.35)	+ 0.14 (1.56)	0.095	0.47	4.88*
3) U	=	0.75 − (7.17)*	0.24* (−2.49)*	+ 0.17 (2.00)*	−0.22) (−2.92)*	0.034 (1.49)					0.093	0.47	6.70*

Note: n = 224; figures in parentheses are t-statistics; * denotes significance at the α = 0.05 level.

Table 6.6

REGRESSIONS ON UNEMPLOYMENT, EXCLUDING THOSE WITH PRIOR TEACHING JOBS

(a) Men and women

(1) U = 1.02 − 0.019 Age − 0.27 Sex + 0.028 Urdu + 0.10 I Matric − 0.044 C.T.
    (2.68)* (−1.39)   (−2.16)*   (1.14)   (1.05)   (−0.50)

$\overline{R}^2$ = 0.029, S.E. estimate = 0.48, F = 2.04, n = 173

(2) U = 0.52 − 0.21 Sex + 0.032 Urdu + 0.12 I Matric
    (4.54)* (−1.82)*   (1.32)   (1.28)

$\overline{R}^2$ = 0.029, S.E. estimate = 0.48, F = 2.74, n = 173

(b) Women only

(1) U = 0.98 − 0.029 Age + 0.027 Urdu + 0.059 I Matric − 0.071 C.T.
    (2.84)* (−1.98)*   (1.04)   (0.55)   (−0.79)

$\overline{R}^2$ = 0.017, S.E. estimate = 0.47, F = 1.65, n = 154

(2) U = 0.83 − 0.023 Age + 0.028 Urdu + 0.072 I Matric
    (2.89)* (−1.83)*   (1.07)   (0.68)

$\overline{R}^2$ = 0.019, S.E. estimate = 0.47, F = 2.00, n = 154

explorations. Some of our findings are given in Table 6.6. Sex remained significant, and the size of the coefficient was about the same. Women were less likely to be employed. Second, the Urdu coefficient stayed about the same size, but the result was no longer statistically significant. Third, having a first-class division in Matric, although still positive in sign, was not statistically significant.[18] Finally, neither age nor degree type (here represented by only a single dummy variable for C.T.) were statistically significant.

We also examined the situation specifically of women who did not have teaching jobs before. In a rather exhaustive exercise, we once again statistically explored the data from the beginning on this sample of 154 female teachers, looking for important variables one-by-one and trying a variety of exploratory regressions. Our 'best' results are given in part (b) of Table 6.6.

Surprisingly, other things being equal, the only consistently important predictor of women's employment was *age;* and this variable had a negative sign. Every regression we tried without age included had adjusted $\bar{R}^2$ of less than one per cent. Even with age included, our *F*-statistics were not impressive. We might be justified in concluding that *none of these variables predicts which newly trained female teachers will get jobs among those who did not have jobs before.*

Other Labour Market Outcomes

Using the same statistical techniques, we studied three other outcomes: teachers' salaries, months of job search between graduation and getting a job, and expressed willingness to work in a rural school. Space only permits the main results; readers may consult our monograph for a full description.

Salaries. Age, months to first job, and type of teaching degree were the only variables to exert a significant effect on salaries (Table 6.7). Other things being equal, the older one was, the higher one's pay—even in a subsample of teachers without a previous teaching job. Those who found jobs sooner tended to have higher paying jobs. Holders of B.Ed. and C.T. degrees had similar salaries, which were greater than the salaries of P.T.C. degree holders. For example, for a

Table 6.7
REGRESSIONS ON SALARY

(a) ln salary = 0.63 + 1.71 ln age − 0.033 months − 0.13 Matric − 0.026 married
              (0.40) (3.42)*   (−1.63)   (−1.62)   (−0.13)

$\bar{R}^2 = 0.23$, S.E. estimate = 0.37, $F = 4.30$, n = 45

(b) ln salary = 2.35 + 1.03 ln age − 0.046 months + 0.28 B.Ed. + 0.32 C.T.
              (1.39) (1.84)*   (2.33)*   (1.95)*   (2.10)*

$\bar{R}^2 = 0.28$, S.E. estimate = 0.36, $F = 5.31$, n = 45

(c) ln salary = 2.80 + 0.97 ln age − 0.040 months − 0.25 P.T.C.
              (1.65) (1.81)*   (−1.89)*   (−1.91)*

$\bar{R}^2 = 0.21$, S.E. estimate = 0.36, $F = 4.55$, n = 42

P.T.C. holder who took six months to find a job and who was twenty-two and a half years old, the predicted monthly salary from equation (b) is Rs 197. For a similar B.Ed. graduate, the predicted salary is Rs 260, and for a similar C.T. degree holder, Rs 271. Even though degree type was not a significant predictor of employment, it did play a role in determining how well paying the job was. Academic performance and specialization did not affect salaries; neither did one's sex.

Length of job search. A histogram of months between graduation and being hired had several spikes, indicating cyclical hiring. None of our many variables were statistically significant predictors of the length of this job search. Perhaps thirteen months is too short a time, or perhaps the job search is simply not affected by academic qualifications, age, or sex.

Willingness to work in rural areas. Nonrespondents to this question looked, on a variety of other dimensions, like those who answered 'no'. We hypothesized that the abnormally high nonresponse rate was really a veiled way of answering in the negative. We did the analyses twice: once omitting the nonresponses and once coding them as 'no'. Table 6.8 gives some of our results at the end of a great deal of exploring. The findings are fairly consistent. Women were less likely to be willing to work in rural areas, non-Urdu speakers more likely, and those with first divisions in Matric less likely. Importantly, neither employment status nor 'seeking work' had any relationship with willingness to work in rural areas (nor did a host of other variables we investigated).

This concludes the description of our many statistical explorations. Our procedures had two virtues: we could avoid decimating our sample (which a regression on all the independent variables would have done, because of differing nonresponse patterns for different variables), and we made quite sure that we did not miss an association if it were there. We gave our predictors 'every chance'. Indeed, the exploratory technique of choosing both the regressions' variables and their transformations on the basis of what we saw biases all of the usual statistics toward significance. That certain

Table 6.8
REGRESSIONS ON 'WOULD WORK IN RURAL AREAS'

(a) Excluding nonresponses

(1) Rural = 0.57 + 0.24 Sex − 0.051 Urdu + 0.21 Matric + 0.061 P.T.C. − 0.070 Unemployed − 0.0089 seeking − 0.061 B.Ed.
     (8.78)** (2.06)* (2.20) (2.22)* (1.02) (−0.90) (−0.34) (−0.61)
$\bar{R}^2 = 0.054$ S.E. estimate = 0.45 $F = 2.25$ n = 154

(2) Rural = 0.52 + 0.24 Sex − 0.053 Urdu + 0.20 I Matric − 0.083 Unemployed
     (4.43)** (2.20)* (−2.31)* (2.12)* (−1.13)
$\bar{R}^2 = 0.063$, S.E. estimate = 0.44, $F = 3.57*$, n = 154

(3) Rural = 0.47 + 0.26 Sex − 0.055 Urdu + 0.19 I Matric
     (4.32)** (2.32)* (−2.39)* (2.00)*
$\bar{R}^2 = 0.061$, S.E. estimate = 0.44, $F = 4.32*$, n = 154

(b) Including nonresponses as 'no' answers

(1) Rural = 0.75 + 0.12 Sex − 0.055 Urdu + 0.13 I Matric − 0.14 Unemployed
     (8.94)** (1.53) (−2.97)** (1.82)* (−2.56)*
$\bar{R}^2 = 0.075$, S.E. estimate = 0.39, $F = 5.52*$, n = 224

(2) Rural = 0.86 − 0.056 Urdu + 0.11 I Matric − 0.16 Unemployed
     (24.31)** (−3.01)** (1.64) (−2.88)**
$\bar{R}^2 = 0.069$, S.E. estimate = 0.39, $F = 6.53*$, n = 224

Note: The figures in parentheses are t-statistics. The dependent variable was coded: 0 = yes, 1 = no. Therefore, a negative sign on a regression coefficient indicates that a positive value on that variable tends to imply a greater likelihood of accepting a rural job. Sex is coded 0 = male, 1 = female; I Matric is coded 0 = no, 1 = yes; unemployment is coded 0 = unemployed, 1 = employed; Urdu is coded 0 = Urdu, 1 = non-Urdu; seeking is coded 0 = yes, 1 = no; *denotes significance at the $\alpha = 0.05$ level; **denotes significance at the $\alpha = 0.01$ level.

variables almost never proved significant—educational qualifications, for example—is thus an even more powerful result.

IV. IMPLICATIONS FOR POLICY

The labour market for teachers was not working well. Many
signs pointed to imbalance and inefficiency. The most
striking: the coexistence of a supposed teacher shortage and
our sample's 55.7 per cent unemployment rate. A rapid
expansion of teacher training in the previous five years had
been accompanied by a decline in real costs per student and,
we were told, by a drop in the quality of the training. The
expansion mostly involved women: in our sample, 87 per
cent were female, compared to an estimated 40 to 60 per
cent several years before. Perhaps as a result, female teachers
had significantly higher unemployment rates.

The problems which we uncovered will not be solved
simply by training more teachers in Karachi. The teacher
shortage was a structural, not an aggregate, phenomenon. The
demand was for rural teachers; the supply was of urban ones.
In Karachi, the demand was greater for men, but the supply
was greater of women.

Our results are also consistent with the proposition that a
merit-based labour market was not in operation. Popular
wisdom said that connections rather than achievements
mattered. We could not disprove this belief.

Sex in the Teacher Market

Our study showed that, holding other relevant factors constant, women have significantly higher unemployment rates
than men. Officials of the School Directorate of Education
reacted to this finding by offering five explanations:[19]

- A teaching career is the most popular career choice for
  educated women, while only a small number of men
  opt for teaching.
- There are more boy's schools than girls'; men teach
  boys and women teach girls.
- Female teachers are reluctant to serve in coeducational
  schools, unlike male teachers.

- Female teachers are less willing than males to teach in rural schools, even those located in the Karachi area.
- Girls who study Science overwhelmingly take the biological/premedical group, in hope of being doctors, which is considered a legitimate profession for women. Those who do not gain entrance into medical college often take up teaching, leading to a glut of female biology teachers and a shortage in the physics/pre-engineering group.

Our quantitative work tended to support these explanations. We found, however, that if women teachers landed a job, they made as much money as male teachers, other things being equal.[20] There may not have been wage discrimination in the labour market—or, indeed, any discrimination at all—but there surely was an odd imbalance between the sexes.[21]

We may usefully note the similarity between the employment situation of women in Pakistan and that of oppressed minorities in other countries. Minority group professionals are often able to obtain jobs only 'among their own kind', as teachers or doctors or dentists serving others in the minority. Jobs in the majority group are taken by majority group members. A segmented labour market with certain self-reinforcing incentives for training and hiring is sometimes in force.

Most well-educated women who work in Pakistan do so 'among their own kind'. One choice is to work at home in one's own household. Another is to work as a teacher or a doctor, and almost invariably such choices involve teaching girls or healing women. It is not clear whether this segmentation results from the preferences of men or of the women themselves; and it will probably not be rewarding to insist upon a single cause for what may be a self-reinforcing, though socially non-optimal, equilibrium.[22] What is clear is that few women are willing to accept rural teaching jobs, to work in boys' schools, or to enter the male-dominated employment areas of business, government service, and the professions, except as they may be working with and for women. For policy purposes, the sexual side of teacher supply and demand is critical. Aggregate projections are not enough.

Geography and Teacher Training

Despite reports of shortages of rural teachers, over half our sample of recently trained Karachi teachers were unemployed and looking for work. However, only 31 per cent of the total sample who answered the question said they would consider a rural job—and many of them were already employed.

Language is one problem. Education in rural Sind is mostly in the Sindhi language. Urdu, as a mother tongue, is spoken by 91 per cent of our sample. The next most widely spoken first language was Punjabi. Language training in Sindhi or Pushto was not a part of teacher training, nor was mother tongue considered when admitting applicants to a teacher training college. Yet in our sample those with non-Urdu mother tongues were significantly more likely to be willing to consider a rural job, other variables held constant.

Several policy issues arise:

- Should resources allocated to the training of urban teachers be shifted to rural areas?
- Should admissions policies favour non-Urdu speakers?
- Should teacher training have a 'rural' element, including language courses?
- Should teachers be required to work two years (say) in rural areas before being considered for urban jobs? Teacher training is heavily subsidized by the State, as we have seen. Could admissions be predicated on a candidate's commitment to accept a rural job after graduation?
- Are there incentives (salary, quarters, transportation, generous leaves) that could induce more teachers, especially women, to take up rural jobs? Could experiments and pilot programmes be attempted to test these incentives?
- Could ways be found to improve the job market for rural teachers—such as combining information from the Directorates of School Education in Hyderabad

and Karachi, removing 'domicile' barriers to hiring, and creating a job bank of unemployed teachers and rural openings?

A *Sifarish*-Based Job Market?

At the end of the *ancien régime* in France, the teachers 'paid by the King' *(gagés du roi)* were still very few. In the southeastern part of the country, teachers were hired at fairs: a man willing to be hired as a teacher would move around with feathers on his hat while crying *maître d'ecole:* one feather meant that the man could teach reading, two feathers meant that he could teach reading and writing and three feathers meant that he could also teach arithmetic. [23]

Pakistan's job market for teachers seems equally bizarre, if less picturesque. Many of our findings are consistent with the idea that the teacher job market works on the basis of *sifarish* (connections) rather than qualifications. This disturbing hypothesis raises broad questions of public policy.

First, we may recapitulate that evidence from our statistical analysis. *No dimensions of the teachers' 'merit' were significant predictors of which ones got jobs:* For example, there was no evidence that receiving a better B.Ed. division, or having first-division Inter standing, or specializing in Science or English, had any significant impact on employability.

Furthermore, *no aspects of a teacher's performance in teacher training college were correlated significantly with salary or with length of job search,* other things being equal.

We investigated the procedures for hiring in an effort to explain these results. Officially, teachers were hired according to two criteria. First, their speciality: did it match the opening at hand? Second, their academic record: did they show excellent achievement?

In practice, however, neither mattered. We learned in interviews in the government and the teacher training institutes that in Karachi virtually every teacher hired in the previous year had been accepted on the basis of a recommendation from a political or official figure. The custom was to consider only those candidates whose applications had been signed by a Minister or other influential person. Even better was a direct phone call from a Minister, which occurred in our presence during the consideration of one applicant, who was hired on the spot. In fact, the Karachi Directorate had not publicly advertised for a teaching position for the previous four years.

Anecdotal evidence was consistent with our statistical findings: the job market for teachers in Karachi seemed to work on connections, not necessarily on competence.

Remedies for such problems are difficult to devise, since the difficulty is by no means unique to this labour market. A systematized, publicly accessible register of openings and candidates is a step worthy of detailed study.

Conclusions

In view of the heavy state subsidy of teacher training and the apparent waste of such a large pool of unemployed urban teachers who were unwilling to take rural jobs, policymakers might consider (1) reducing the number of teachers trained in Karachi, in favour of expanded rural training facilities; (2) raising tuitions to cover at least the recurring costs; and (3) an agreement by all entering teachers to take a rural job upon graduation, for a specified number of years. In the absence of a radical change in labour market conditions, teacher training policies in Karachi were ill serving teachers, students, and taxpayers.

NOTES

[1] Robert E. Klitgaard, *et al.* *The Economics of Teacher Training,* Research Report No.8, Applied Economics Research Centre, University of Karachi, January 1977.

[2] John W. Tukey, *Exploratory Data Analysis,* Addison-Wesley, Reading, Mass., 1977, pp. 1-3.

[3] We cannot, therefore, use the brute force, exploratory regression techniques proposed by Cuthbert Daniel and Fred Wood, *Fitting Equations to Data,* Wiley, New York, 1971, which analyse the results of regressions on every possible combination of independent variables and some of their transformations.

[4] See, for example, H.J. Larson and T.A. Bancroft, 'Sequential Model Building for Prediction in Regression Analysis, I', *Annals of Mathematical Statistics,* Vol. 34, 1963, pp 462-79; N.R. Draper and H. Smith, *Applied Regression Analysis,* John Wiley and Sons, New York, 1966; and T.A. Bancroft, 'Analysis and Inference for Incompletely Specified Models Involving the Use of Preliminary Test(s) of Significance', *Biometrica,* Vol. 20, 1964, pp. 427-42.

[5] As a rough rule of thumb, in multiple regression analysis one likes to have $n-k > 75$, where n is the number of observations and k is the number of independent variables.

[6] When the analyst considers many alternative specifications and chooses according to a criterion like 'smallest residual variance', his or her resulting estimate of that variance will, on the average, be below the true figure.

[7] See, for example, Marc Nerlove and S.J. Press, *Unvariable and Multivariate Log-Linear and Logistic Models*, R–1306–EDA/NIH, The Rand Corporation, Santa Monica, Calif., 1973; Max Halperin, William C. Blackwelder, and Joel I. Verter, 'Estimation of the Multivariate Logistic Risk Function: A Comparison of the Discriminant Function and Maximum Likelihood Approaches', *Journal of Chronic Diseases*, Vol. 24, 1971, pp. 125-58.

[8] For a comparison of the logit specification with other models, see Yvonne M.M. Bishop, Stephen E. Fienberg, and Paul W. Holland, *Discrete Multivariate Analysis: Theory and Practice,* Cambridge, Mass., MIT Press, 1975, chapters 2 and 3, pp. 366-72. They summarize:'Lest the reader conclude that the only problem remaining is to make an intelligent choice of existing methods, we now indicate the urgent need for the development of further methodology ... [M]uch ... remains to be done, particularly when the data base is large and consists of mixed variables, and measurements are unevenly replicated', p. 371.

[9] If the same linear combination of independent variables for teachers with $R_i=1$ are all larger or smaller than the corresponding values for teachers with $R_i=0$, the maximum likelihood estimates for the logit parameters will not exist.

[10] A.M. Kshirsagar, *Multivariate Analysis*, Marcel Dekker, New York, 1972, p. 213.

[11] Halperin, Blackwelder, and Verter, op.cit.; unpublished work by Gus Haggstrom and others at the Rand Corporation; and some of the examples analysed in Nerlove and Press, op. cit., who, nonetheless, argue in favour of MLE estimators. The logit parameter α_1 is estimated by multiplying the OLS regression coefficient by $n/SS_{\hat{e}}$, where SS_e is the residual sum of squares.

[12] Admission requirements for these degree programmes help describe who participates in each:

	Age	Academic qualification
M.Ed.	none	B.Ed., D.P.E.
B.Ed.	none	Bachelor's degree
P.T.C.	16 to 22	Matric (secondary)
C.T.	19 to 22	Inter (higher secondary)

[13] No general rules of thumb exist about the likely size or distribution of non-response bias. 'There is now ample evidence that these biases vary considerably from item to item and from survey to survey, being sometimes negligible and sometimes large' (William G. Cochran, *Sampling Techniques*, second edition, New York, 1963, p. 389).

[14] Y.M.M. Bishop, S.E. Fienberg, and P.W. Holland, op. cit., p. 124.

[15] This calculation includes the 262 who gave answers about employment status, sex, and age; it includes those in college as jobless.

[16] The dummy for 'lived with parents' was coded 0 = yes, 1 = no.

[17] To represent degree types, we omitted the one M.Ed. degree holder and created two dummy variables, one for B.Ed. and one for P.T.C. The dummy for 'had teaching job before teacher training college was coded 0=yes, 1=no.

18 We hypothesize that first divisioners in Matric were more likely to have had a teaching job *before* and *after* teacher training college.

19 Interviews, January and February 1977.

20 That is, given equal credentials, ages, and so forth. However, women tended to dominate in the relatively poorly paid C.T. degree programme, while most of the men were in the relatively well-paid B.Ed. programme. Other things were not equal.

21 It is sometimes said that most female teacher training students are not serious about working—that they simply marry upon graduation and do not enter the labour force. Our study does not support this idea. Over 95 per cent of the women were seeking jobs or were employed, and under 10 per cent were married.

22 In such an equilibrium the preferences of members of both the dominant and minority group may lead to an unequal outcome. It may be empirically impossible using data on outcomes to differentiate among the large variety of analytically possible causes. In particular, to lay exclusive blame on employer discrimination in the job market may overlook the deeper structure of inequality. See Gary Becker, *The Economics of Discrimination*, second edition, Chicago, 1971; and Robert E. Klitgaard, 'Institutionalized Racism: An Analytic Approach', *Journal of Peace Research*, Vol. 8, No. 1, 1972.

23 Carlo Cipolla, *Literacy and Development in the West*, Penguin, Middlesex, England, 1969, pp. 29-30.

CHAPTER 7

WHO SHOULD GO TO UNIVERSITY?

Statistical findings can be misleading; the importance of a statistical result depends on the context in which decisions are made. This chapter illustrates this point with regard to the result of correlation analysis. In the context of selective admissions, what seems to be a 'low' correlation coefficient may not imply an unimportant statistical relationship. The chapter also introduces the concepts of the reliability of measurement and of restriction of range. Multiple regression analysis is also employed.

In most countries of the developing world, students are chosen for higher education on the basis of examination results.[1] In the People's Republic of China, for example, about one in every twenty applicants to the university is admitted, chosen on the basis of scores on an entrance test. In Indonesia, a special multiple choice examination lasting two days is used to select university students.

Pakistan is no exception. The Intermediate (or 'Inter') examinations after grade twelve assess how much students learned in secondary school and also determine students' chances of continuing their education. How well students do on examinations becomes a major determinant of their life chances.

Is it a good idea for universities to rely so heavily on examination results? A lot hinges on these test scores. Later income and years of education are closely related. True, a university degree is neither necessary nor sufficient for becoming rich or powerful.[2] But doctors, engineers, and pharmacists usually occupy high positions on the socio-economic ladder—and the only way in Pakistan to have a chance of becoming a doctor, lawyer, or engineer is by doing well on the Inter Exams.

Exam scores shape individual destinies; obviously, universities are also affected by this system of selecting students.

This chapter was written by Robert Klitgaard. W. Eric Gustatson, Muneer A. Khan, Sadequa Dadabhoy, Shamsia Islam, and Javed Iqbal assisted in the collection and analysis of the data.

Society cares, too. Somehow, society must decide how to select from many applicants those who will become its future doctors, engineers, and leaders. Only about a tenth of the applicants to Karachi's Institute of Business Administration can be accepted. The fractions are almost as small at Karachi's professional colleges of engineering, medicine, and pharmacy. Society also cares who is selected because it pays most of the educational bills. The students accepted in public universities contribute less than 10 per cent of the true costs of their education; the government subsidizes the rest. Failure rates are high—26 per cent in engineering college, for example, and 37 per cent in medical college.[3] Consequently, the social costs of admitting the wrong students are large.

The *efficiency* of the admissions process therefore becomes an important subject of public policy. Admission has many dimensions besides efficiency, such as bias, fairness, the incentives it creates, and the costs of the selection system. Clearly, many issues of social justice are involved, which transcend statistical analysis. These other dimensions will be discussed briefly at the end of the chapter. But for the most part we shall confine our attention to a narrow and important question, which is intimately intertwined with data analysis: How efficient is the selection system? We shall focus our attention on the affiliated institutions of the University of Karachi in the mid-seventies.

Admissions Policies

The several parts of the University of Karachi that we shall study based admission on what might be called 'intellectual merit'. Their specific policies differed in detail, but the broad features were as follows:

- A student's Inter score, based on an exam taken after twelfth grade, was the most important, and in some cases the sole, criterion for admission.
- Occasionally, very superior performance in the tenth-grade Matric Exam would be considered as a positive factor.
- A few seats were reserved for students from far-flung

areas, from scheduled castes, with athletic talent, or with a parent on the university faculty.
- Only in the case of the Business Institute were interviews used and crude IQ tests employed.

Notice that intellectual merit is defined in terms of performance on examinations. To my knowledge, no explicit formulation of the reasons for relying almost exclusively on this criterion has been made in Pakistan.

Presumably, the reasons would rest on *predictive validity*. A test is said to have predictive validity if scores on it correctly anticipate future results of interest. Thus, Inter marks have predictive validity for academic performance if they can predict who will do well and who will do badly at higher levels of education. If examination marks are poor predictors of University success, presumably the argument for using them as the admission criterion is greatly weakened.

How can we assess the value of using a predictor, such as test scores? In what follows, a statistical analysis is presented of how well the current examination system predicts later academic success. We will also develop a framework that enables us to answer such questions as:

- How much would society lose if admission were done by lot instead of by the current examinations?
- How much would it be worth to develop a better predictor—say, an improved examination or the addition of other information in the admissions system?

The Strategy and the Data

How well do students' scores in Inter Exams foretell their later University success? If Inter marks (I) predict later University performance (P), we expect the correlation between them to be positive and statistically significant. As I goes up, we expect P to go up. Intuitively, many of us may feel that if I is to be the sole criterion for admission, I should 'explain' much of the variance observed in P.

These questions naturally lend to the computation of

correlation coefficients and regression equations. The sample correlation between I and P is:

$$r = \frac{\Sigma(I_i - \bar{I})(P_i - \bar{P})}{n\, s_I\, s_p}$$

where I_i is the Inter score of the individual i, $\bar{I}$ is the mean score in the sample on the Inter test. P_i is the performance in the university of individual i, $\bar{P}$ is the mean of university performance in the sample, n is the number of students in the sample, s_I is the sample standard deviation of Inter scores, and s_p is the sample standard deviation of university performance.

The correlation coefficient r is a measure of the strength of the linear relationship between two variables. It can take values between -1.0 and $+1.0$, where -1.0 indicates a perfectly negative linear relationship, 0 no linear relationship, and $+1.0$ indicates a perfectly positive linear relationship.

Closely related to correlation analysis is linear regression analysis. In the simplest case, we try to predict P using a single variable I:

$$\hat{P} = \hat{\beta}_0 + \hat{\beta}_1\, I,$$

where $\hat{\beta}_0$ and $\hat{\beta}_1$ are constants.[4] The estimated regression coefficient $\hat{\beta}_1$ tells us, roughly speaking, how much of a change in predicted performance $\hat{P}$ is associated with a one-point increase in the Inter score.

These sorts of correlations and regressions were computed for the institutions in the study. When possible, the effect on University performance of supposedly 'extraneous' factors—such as sex, rural or urban residence, father's education, possession of a telephone, and primary school's medium of instruction—was also examined. Here, the statistical tool was multiple regression analysis. The regression coefficients tell, roughly speaking, how much of a change in performance is associated with a one-unit change in each independent variable, after statistically adjusting for the other independent variables.

As will become evident, the data analysed were not as extensive or as detailed as one would wish. Each data set was laboriously assembled, often from untabulated sheets, and each has its limitations, be it sample size or the number of variables on which information is available. But the data do enable us to assess the predictive validity of the prevailing criteria of intellectual merit.

Pharmacy, Medicine and Engineering

In these three professional programmes, the Inter score was the sole admissions criterion for twelfth-grade applicants. How well did this score 'predict' a student's eventual success?

To find out, we collected information on groups of recent graduates:

- For the pharmacy college, we obtained data for 110 graduates of the class of 1974 on final pharmacy marks (P), Inter marks (I), and Matric marks (M).
- For the Dow Medical College, we collected data on 89 students who appeared in the final professional M.B.B.S. examination, held in February 1975. The information included medical score (Medic), I, M, sex, and residence in Karachi or not (K).
- For the N.E.D., Engineering University, we assembled data on 186 students who appeared in the B.E. examination 1972, held in 1973. The variables were engineering score (E), speciality (electrical, mechanical, or civil engineering), I, and M.[5]

Presumably higher Inter scores lead to higher performance —the relationship P = f(I) is monotonically increasing. But we had no *a priori* notion of the exact functional form (linear, logarithmic, quadratic, etc.), nor of exactly how other variables should be taken into account. Therefore, regression analysis was used as an *exploratory* tool. One begins with a linear model, examines residual plots, and attempts what seem to be more suitable specifications of the regression equation. (These ideas are described more fully in chapters 1, 2, and 6.)

Table 7.1 gives the results of simple linear regression with Inter marks as the independent variable.[6]

Residual plots for pharmacy and for medical colleges did not indicate curvilinearity, and alternative functional forms (logarithmic and quadratic, for pharmacy; logarithmic for medicine) did not perform better than the simple linear equation. For the engineering college, however, a scatterplot indicated a nonlinear relationship between E and I; in later regressions on E, a quadratic function was used.

Several findings in Table 7.1 stand out. First, the regression coefficients on I were similar in the three equations. A student with a ten-point higher Inter score was predicted to have a score about three or four percentage points higher in a professional college. Second, the t-statistics were all statistically significant beyond the α = 0.01 level. That is, performance and I were significantly correlated, as expected.

But, third, *the percentage of variance explained by I seemed low.* The R^2 in the linear specifications ranged from 0.055 in engineering college to 0.16 in medical college; from 5.5 to 16 per cent of the variance was explained by I. Most of the variation in professional college performance could not be statistically explained by the Inter scores.

The results can be stated in another way. Within the range of scores examined here, a student's Inter score did not precisely forecast his or her later success. For example take a pharmacy student with an Inter score of 531. Our best guess of his or her subsequent pharmacy score is 490, but there is a 33 per cent chance that the true score is outside the rather large range of 435 to 524.[7] Notice that the standard deviation of P is 37.3; the standard error of our estimate of P_i knowing

Table 7.1
SIMPLE REGRESSIONS FOR PHARMACY, MEDICAL
AND ENGINEERING COLLEGES

Score	Constant	Inter coefficient	n	$\overline{R}^2$	r	S.E. estimate
P	322.9	0.31 (4.4)**	110	0.15	0.39	34.4
Medic	38.1	0.33 (4.2)**	99	0.16	0.40	7.05
E	37.0	0.39 (3.4)**	186	0.055	0.23	10.87

** Indicates significance at the α = 0.01 level.
Note: Figures in parentheses are t-statistics.

I_i is 34.4, which is a 'reduction in our uncertainty' of less than 8 per cent.

One might think that if an applicant's Matric score (M) were also taken into account, one could make a better prediction of P. With this thought in mind, numerous multiple regressions were run, using residual analyses to help discover the 'best fit'. The coefficients of M (or M^2) were not statistically significant at the $\alpha = 0.05$ level, except at the medical college. Moreover, the percentage of variation explained rose only a little. Even with Intermediate and Matric scores used simultaneously as predictors, very little of the variance in professional college performance could be explained.

Further analyses looked at additional independent variables (including sex, region of residence, and father's education). None of them was a statistically significant predictor of later academic performance, once the Inter score was taken into account.

The Business Institute

Statistical explorations on a richer data set for the Institute of Business Administration followed the same exploratory strategy. Numerous simple and multiple regressions were tried. Plots and residual analyses from each were examined, and subsequent changes in the specification were carried out. In effect, examination scores were 'given every chance' to demonstrate how well they predicted academic performance at IBA. The results are not presented here; basically, they showed that none of the independent variables reached statistical significance at conventional levels. In particular, Inter scores were not statistically significantly associated with later marks.

The Faculties of Arts and Sciences

The richest data set and most exhaustive statistical analyses concerned admissions to the University of Karachi's Faculties of Arts and Science. A stratified sample of 2,786 students was selected from the class of 1971 in a remarkable data gathering effort by Rabia Raffi from the University's own records. Available variables included division obtained from the University in 1971 (i.e. first, second, third, pass), Inter division, Matric division, sex, certain proxies for socio-economic status (father's education, has telephone or not), and an indicator of command of English (medium of instruction in the student's primary school).

Important statistical problems emerge with the analysis of discrete dependent variable and with ordinal independent variables : space does not allow an elaboration of the problems or our solutions to them, but some of the issues are taken up in chapter 6. Neither shall the elaborate statistical explorations of these data be detailed here. Table 7. 2 provides a qualitative summary of the 'best-fitting' equations for different subject areas.

The low percentages of variation explained by these regressions reinforce the results from the professional colleges. Even after including Matric division, father's education, sex, primary school medium, and possession of a telephone as independent variables, the regressions have little predictive power. The Inter score itself is not statistically significant in three of the five equations, when the other predictors are 'held constant'.

Table 7.2
PREDICTORS FOR DIFFERENT SUBJECT AREAS,
FACULTIES OF ARTS AND SCIENCES

		Predictors							
Subject	N	Inter	Matric	Sex	Medium	Father's education	Telephone	$\overline{R}^2$	r	F
All arts	1160	*	n.s.	*	*	*	n.s.	0.09	0.30	27.13
All sciences	423	n.s.	*	n.s.	n.s.	n.s.	*	0.02	0.14	5.22
Engineering	33	n.s.	n.s.	n.s.	n.s.	n.s.	n.s.	0.26	0.51	1.93
Education	66	n.s.	n.s.	n.s.	n.s.	n.s.	n.s.	0.04	0.20	2.02
Commerce	204	*	n.s.	n.s.	n.s.	n.s.	n.s.	0.07	0.26	15.15

Note: *Signifies significance at the 0.05 level with the anticipated sign (including that girls do better than boys); n.s. signifies not significant. The Commerce equation used logarithms for division status (1, 2, 3, or pass) at the university, Inter, and Matric levels.

Interpreting the Results

How can we link these statistical findings to the question of the efficiency of the current selection system? Let us focus upon the pharmacy college as our primary example.

It looks at first as though the examinations are quite inefficient. After all, they explain such a small amount of the variance in later performance. Since the R^2 in the pharmacy equation was 0.15, then 100 per cent–15 per cent, or 85 per cent of the variance in academic performance at the pharmacy college was *not* explained by marks on the Inter examinations. The correlation coefficient was only 0.39. Do not these findings invalidate the argument for using the examinations, by showing how weakly they are related to later performance?

Supporting this appraisal was a small study several colleagues and I carried out at the University of Karachi in 1976. Both Inter marks and later measures of performance are subject to several kinds of unreliability. One has to do with differences in judgement among graders: it is called 'inter-rater unreliability'. Most examinations in Pakistan, including the Inter and Matric Exams were not 'objective' in the sense of multiple choice or true-false questions. Different graders mark different tests, and despite guidelines for grading each answer, no two graders mark exactly alike.

How much did graders tend to differ? To find out, with the co-operation of the Matric Exam authorities, my colleagues and I obtained the actual examination booklets submitted by a sample of students in four subjects in the previous year. We also selected a random sample of graders of these examinations, from a master list of all graders in the previous year. We invited these graders to the University and paid them for their help. The sample of examination books was then graded independently by several graders. The average of the correlations of the marks given by different graders to the same answers was 0.7. Obviously, this result shows that some of the variation in Matric scores is made up of inter-rater unreliability, and this of course limits the ability of the examination to predict later performance.

A similar lack of inter-rater reliability would probably be found for the Inter test and in the performance measures used by universities.[8] A lack of reliability *in the predictor* is a sign of a poor predictor. But if the *performance measure* itself is unreliable, meaning that it contains random error that no predictor can be expected to forecast, then we may want to adjust our estimation of how well a predictor does. This subject quickly leads us into a thicket of complexities which, for present purposes, we need not enter. Suffice it to say that we should not necessarily judge a *predictor* to be faulty because the measure of later performance is unreliable. Statisticians have developed an 'adjusted' correlation coefficient, which 'corrects' for criterion unreliability. The formula for this correction is:

$$r_{adj} = \frac{r}{\sqrt{rel.}}$$

where r is the correlation coefficient and rel. is the reliability coefficient of the measure to be predicted.[9]

For the pharmacy college, this calculation would lead to a higher correlation. If the reliability of pharmacy marks were 0.7, then:

$$r_{adj} = 0.39 / \sqrt{0.7} = 0.47$$

We should note this point: Some of the problem of inaccurate prediction resides in inaccurate measures of outcomes, rather than in poor predictors. Unadjusted correlation coefficients understate how well predictors really do.

Restriction of Range

There is another reason why our correlations are low. We obviously have only been able to analyse the performance of those applicants who were actually admitted. These are the people who scored highest on the Inter Exams. The variation in Inter scores in this restricted sample is much less than the variation among all students who took the Inter Exam. Consequently, the correlation between Inter scores and later performance is lower than it would be for the whole population of test-takers.

Again, many statistical complexities enter, which we should not allow to obscure the basic point: we need to be very careful in extrapolating our results from a sample of people who are all very high on the predictor to the entire population of applicants. Notice that it is this entire population of candidates that concerns us when we ask whether examination scores are a good device for selecting university students. We need somehow to adjust the observed correlation among the selected sample so that it reflects the correlation that would be observed in the whole population of applicants, were they all to be accepted to university. Under assumptions of linearity and homoscedasticity[10] in the relationship between the predictor and the performance measure, the adjustment formula is:

$$r_{adj} = \frac{r^* \, (\sigma/\sigma^*)}{\sqrt{1 - r^{*2} + r^{*2} \, (\sigma^2/\sigma^{*2})}}$$

where r^* is the correlation between Inter marks and later performance within the selected group, σ is the standard deviation of Inter scores in the entire test-taking population, and σ^* is the standard deviation of Inter scores within the selected group.[11]

If $\sigma/\sigma^* = 2$, as it may well be in highly selective situations like the pharmacy college and the other institutions we have studied, and $r^* = 0.39$, then $r_{adj} = 0.65$. This is a considerable increase.

The Efficiency of a Predictor

Still, one might respond, are Inter scores really efficient in predicting later academic performance? Let us continue with the pharmacy case as an example. Even after adjusting for both unreliability in the later performance measure and for restriction of range,[12] r is 0.73, which means that R^2 is only 0.53. This leaves 47 per cent of the variance in performance unexplained. Compared to many other economic and statistical problems on which one might work, this may seem rather a low R^2.

But there is no rule that tells us that a certain R^2 is 'low' or 'high'. It depends on the problem. It turns out that, in our problem of selecting a few students from a large applicant

118   DATA ANALYSIS FOR DEVELOPMENT

pool, *even a relatively modest increase in r (or R^2) can lead to large gains in efficiency.* Let us see why this is so.

Consider the simplest linear regression for an individual's performance P in pharmacy college:

(1) $P = \mu_p + \beta Z_I + e,$

where μ_p is the mean later performance of *randomly selected* group of applicants, Z_I is the student's Inter score *I* expressed in standardized scores (or z-scores),[13] and e is the error term.

What is the average performance *of the selected group* of applicants? It is:

(2) $E(P_s) = E(\mu_p) + E(\beta Z_{Is}) + E(e),$

where the subscript s means 'in the selected group'. Since $E(e) = 0$ and μ_p and β are constants, this becomes:

(3) $\bar{P}_s = \mu_p + \beta\bar{Z}_{Is}$

Since $\beta = r(\sigma_p/\sigma_I)$, where σ_p is the standard deviation in later peformance in pharmacy college of a *randomly selected* group of applicants, and since we have normalized the Inter scores so that $\sigma_I = \sigma_{zI} = 1$, then $\beta = r\sigma_p$. We thereby obtain:

(4) $\bar{P}_s = \mu_p + r\sigma_p\bar{Z}_{Is}$

How can we use this formula to assess the efficiency of doing the selection with the Inter Exam? We might compare the average performance of the selected fraction of applicants in two situations: first where the Inter Exam is used to do the choosing, second where instead students are selected randomly from the applicant pool. In the second case, the expected performance in the pharmacy college $\bar{P}_s$ is just μ_p. The first case is described by equation (4). Therefore, the gain in expected performance in the selected group from using the examination is $r\sigma_p\bar{Z}_{Is}$.

(5) $\Delta\bar{P}$ per selectee $= r\sigma_p\bar{Z}_{Is}.$

Let us examine equation (5) term by term.

Notice that the r here is the correlation between the Inter score and later performance in pharmacy college in the entire applicant pool. It is the r we observe in the already selected sample after correcting for restriction of range. As shown above, for the pharmacy college, this r_{adj} = 0.65. (If we also adjusted for unreliability, r_{adj} = 0.73; but let us use the 0.65 figure for simplicity's sake.)

What is $\overline{Z}_{Is}$? This is the expected Inter score of a selected student. If Inter scores are normally distributed and the proportion selected is π, then it can be shown that:

$$(6) \quad \overline{Z}_{Is} = \phi/\pi,$$

where ϕ is the ordinate of the standard normal distribution corresponding to a π chance of being selected.[14]

What about σ_p? Recall that this is the standard deviation in a pharmacy college performance of a randomly selected group of students. The standard deviation in performance that we actually observe among the students selected via the Inter Exam will be smaller than σ_p. Alas, in the absence of an experiment, we cannot observe σ_p. But we can make a few assumptions about it, do some sensitivity analysis, and obtain some useful results.

For example, let's be conservative and set σ_p equal to the standard deviation in P that we now observe among selected students. Ask yourself this: how much is a standard deviation increase in performance in the pharmacy college worth to society, in rupees? If we could magically improve a pharmacy student's final performance from the fiftieth percentile to the eighty-fourth percentile—this is about one standard deviation in a normal distribution—how much would this be worth to society?

You can use a number or two of your choice. Let me arbitrarily give the number Rs 20,000 per student. I think it might be even higher, although I don't know how I might prove this. But using this as the value in rupees of σ_p, we can calculate the efficiency (in rupee terms per student) of using the examination to select pharmacy students as opposed to selecting students at random. We do so as follows. Suppose:

$r = 0.39 \quad r_{adj} = 0.65$

$\pi = 0.125$; here we suppose that one in eight students is selected

ϕ corresponding to $(\pi = 0.125) = 0.272$

$\bar{Z}_{Is} = \phi/\pi = 0.272/0.125 = 2.18$

$\sigma_p = Rs \ 20,000$

Then $r \ \sigma_p \ \phi/\pi = 0.65 \ 20,000 \ . \ 2.18 = Rs \ 28,340$ is the gain per student that is obtained by selecting with the examination as opposed to selecting randomly. If we have 200 students, the gain is 200. 28,340 = Rs 56,68,000 per year.

A number of assumptions are embedded in this analysis, including linearity, homoscedasticity, and normality. But the general idea shines through. *Even with a relatively low R^2, the use of the Inter Exam leads to sizeable improvements in the efficiency of selection.*

This same statistical methodology could be used to address other questions. For example, how much would it be worth to improve the exam, so that the unadjusted correlation would go from 0.39 to, say, 0.50? (Answer: Rs 4,620 per selected student.) How much would it be worth to use additional information that would increase the multiple correlation R by a certain amount? If enrollments are doubled so that the selection ratio π is halved, how much would then be gained by using the examinations instead of selecting at random? (Answer: Rs 16,510) per student selected.)

Conclusions

As noted earlier in the chapter, admissions policies have many important dimensions. Individuals and society as a whole care about the efficiency of selection, defined in terms of choosing those who will be most likely to do well in their future studies, thereby reducing the social costs of failures. We may also care about a broader definition of efficiency, one going well beyond the prediction of academic performance alone. Is the selection system admitting those for whom the social value-added of higher education is greatest?

We also may care about the effect of various selection systems on particular groups in the society. Does an examination in English or Urdu unfairly exclude disproportionate numbers of Sindhi or Baluchi or Pushto speakers? Do examinations exclude 'too many' poor people or people from rural areas or females or . . . ?

And then the choice of selection systems—examinations or otherwise—creates incentives going back to previous stages of the educational system. Because the marks are used as the criterion for admission to higher levels, students invest their energies in the procurement of marks, which in turn presumably increases the amount they learn. (Shortly we shall consider the possibility of adverse incentives generated by marks.) Apart from their possible predictive power, high school marks also have *productive* power, in terms of invoking certain behaviour at pre-University levels of education.

Presumably, eliminating marks as a criterion for University admissions would also reduce their power to motivate high school students. Many college teachers and educational officials have expressed the importance of this incentive. 'If we got rid of marks', one said, 'my students would do no work at all'. Marks are said to motivate students for two reasons: first, to graduate from high school; and second, for many but not all, to qualify for higher education. Even if marks could be shown to have no predictive validity, most teachers would probably oppose the abandonment of marks in admissions policy, because of these incentive effects.

This productive power, however, is sometimes used as an argument *against* marks. Critics contend that marks provide adverse incentives outweighing the good ones: students invest too much time in the wrong kinds of learning activities. Michael Spence explains:

> From reasonably early ages, students are guided through courses of study designed to make them look like good bets (lotteries) to colleges. The expenditure of student effort, and the concomitant anxiety over a long period, may constitute a large diversion of human resources and energies away from relatively productive activities at earlier ages.[15]

Spence goes on to show, with plausible theoretical models, that students' overinvestment in marks-producing behaviour may distort the predictive or signaling power of marks, thus adding another overlay of inefficiency to the situation.

What are the facts about incentive effects in Pakistan? Matric and Inter Exams are often said to stress the wrong things and therefore to induce students to do so, too. A 1956 report by the Board of Secondary Education in Lahore did not mince words:

> The dead weight of the examination has tended to curb the teachers' initiative, to stereotype the curriculum, to promote mechanical and lifeless methods of teaching, to discourage all spirit of experimentation and to place the stress on wrong or unimportant things in education.[16]

A. Haque concurs:

> Not only pupils but teachers are affected by the present system of examination . . . Examinations dictate curriculum instead of following it, and hamper the proper treatment of the subjects and sound method of teaching.[17]

Mohammad Basharat Ali believes that making marks a less important factor in admissions policy will have favourable results:

> The results of any public examination at the end of any stage like SSC, HSC, etc. should not be treated as 'passport' for admission to the next higher stage. There must be arrangements devised at any academic stage for selection/rejection of students. This gives the academic institutions opportunity to screen students the way they want. It also furnishes the students with the understanding that the result of any public examination is not all that they should have to do with but they may face other trials to get into the next academic programme. This will surely cut down much of the unusually wrong and pernicious attitude sustained by the student towards final examinations.[18]

Expert opinions like these notwithstanding, hard evidence on the incentive effects of examinations is not plentiful, in Pakistan as elsewhere. Much anecdotal evidence, indeed, indicates that students underinvest in study at all levels of education in Pakistan.

We should also consider the incentives that might be created were examinations to be abolished. The case of the People's Republic of China is instructive. In 1966, at the outset of the Cultural Revolution, the government banned entrance examinations. Instead, students were to be selected for higher education by cadres of workers, peasants, and soldiers, through the Communist Party. The criteria emphasized 'correct' political views, revolutionary dedication, and the 'right' social class origin. But the new procedures led to some awkward results, including what the Chinese call 'getting in the back door': namely, the use of· political influence and occasionally direct corruption to obtain admissions for one's son or daughter.[19]

In general, a selection system based on subjective judgements is more prone to corruption, influence, and *sifarish*. A system based on objective performance—such as an examination system—does not create as many such incentives. In some circumstances, this aspect of a selection procedure can be crucial.

A final dimension of selection systems is their cost. This includes the cost of preparing and grading the examinations, the direct and opportunity costs incurred by students taking the exams, and the cost of students' having to wait for their examination results to be announced. In Pakistan in the mid-seventies, it often took six months for the essay examinations to be graded and the results compiled and announced. Presumably, this led many aspirants to delay their entry into the job market, thereby creating opportunity costs. In contrast, Indonesia's multiple choice test takes only two weeks to grade, compile and announce.

These are all important dimensions of any choice regarding admissions policies. The statistical analysis presented here provides only part of the answer. Nonetheless, several interesting findings have emerged:

- At several faculties, Inter scores are not statistically significant predictors of later academic performance. The search should commence, therefore, for better examinations or for other predictors that might be used in admissions.
- Regression analysis enables one to interpret examination scores (and other predictors) more meaningfully. For the three professional colleges of medicine, pharmacy, and engineering, we learned that a ten-point increase in

the Inter score corresponds to about a 3 percentage point increase in later academic performance. We saw that, after controlling for the Inter score, various measures of socio-economic background were not statistically significant predictors of later performance.

• Even a relatively low R^2 or correlation coefficient may not say much about the usefulness of a predictor. In the case of a very selective admissions system, using a predictor with a 'low' correlation of 0.2 or 0.3 can still lead to a great gain in efficiency compared to random selection. A simplistic use of 'percentage of variance explained' or 'significantly correlated' can mislead us badly.

The choice of admissions policies is a matter that transcends statistical analysis. But presumably whatever one's political or ethical values, one can make better decisions by having statistical results like ours.

NOTES

1 This is also true in the industrialized West: 'The fact remains that, in spite of all criticisms concerning the use of school records and/or standardized tests as bases for selection, they continue practically everywhere to be decisive in determining the chances of qualified students to proceed directly to higher education and even more so in being admitted to the institutions or streams of their choice'. (Dorotea Furth, 'Selection and Equity: An International Viewpoint', *Comparative Education Review*, Vol. 22 No. 2, June 1978, p. 270.)

2 Many members of Pakistan's economic elite, for example, have had little formal education; see Gustav Papanek, *Pakistan's Development Experience II*, Harvard University Press, Cambridge, Mass., 1970.

3 Based on 1974 data from the N.E.D. Engineering University and the Dow Medical College.

4 In the case of univariate regression, β_1 is related to the correlation coefficient r

$$\hat{\beta} = r(\sigma_P/\sigma_s)$$

5 For medical and engineering students who failed the examination—37 per cent of the medical students and 26 per cent of the engineering students—no marks are given, just a fail. We coded the failures as the maximum failing score, 49 marks for medicine and 45 marks for engineering.

6 Note that the pharmacy equation defines both dependent and independent variables as ten times the percentage score—these are the so-called 'marks'—whereas, in the equations or engineering and medicine, percentage scores are used.

7 That is, $\hat{P}\pm$ standard error of the estimate is 490 ± 34.4 for I = 531. Our 95 per cent confidence interval on P given I = 531 is 490 ± 68.8, or from 431.2 to 558.8.

8 In the United States, for example, studies have shown a reliability coefficient of about 0.45 for a single college test and perhaps 0.80 for a semester's grade-point

average. These are broader measures than just the inter-rater reliability. (Robert L. Ebel, *Essentials of Educational Measurement*, Prentice-Hall, Englewood Cliffs, N.J., 1972; Loren Spencer Barritt, 'Note: The Consistency of First-Semester College Grade-point Average', *Journal of Educational Measurement*, Vol. 3, No. 2, Fall 1966, p. 1262). In England, similar results have been obtained: 'There is abundant evidence that examinations of the so-called *essay-type*, used in this country and elsewhere, tend to be intrinsically unreliable'. (W. D. Furneaux, *The Chosen Few: An Examination of Some Aspects of University Selection in Britain*, Oxford University Press, London, 1961, pp. 94-5.)

9 The formula depends on certain simplifying assumptions; see Frederic M. Lord and Melvin R. Novick, *Statistical Theories of Mental Test Scores*, Addison-Wesley, Reading, Mass., 1968, chapter 6.

10 Is the predictive relationship really linear for all levels of test scores? It is, of course, hard to say without an experiment that would actually admit some low-scoring students. I would guess that Inter third divisioners and those merely passing would, if admitted to the university, do less well than an extrapolation of our findings would lead us to predict. For example, from the large data set on the University of Karachi's Faculties of Arts and Sciences, it was found that the probability of securing a first-class degree given that one had a first-class Inter score was 0.13. For those having second-class Inter scores, the probability of a University first division was only slightly lower, 0.11. But for students with third-class Inter scores, the probability of securing a first-class University degree dropped to only 0.03. On the other hand, some old data from the Institute of Business Administration showed that the probability of completing IBA studies successfully was higher for third-division B.Sc. holders than for first-division B.Sc. holders. (The situation was reversed for B.A. holders.) See West Pakistan Institute of Management, 'A Study of Significant Aspects of Success and Failure Among IBA Candidates: 1962-6', processed, no date.

11 For a review of the technicalities, see Lord and Novick, ibid., pp.140-8.

12 In these calculations, the realibility of pharmacy marks was assumed to be 0.7 and σ/σ^* was assumed to be 2.

13 The standardized score Z_I is calculated by subtracting the average Inter score in the applicant pool and dividing by the standard deviation of Inter scores in the applicant pool:

$$Z_I = \frac{I - \mu_I}{\sigma_I}$$

14 For example, if one in five applicants is selected, $\pi = 0.20$. Look in statistical tables to find the value of ϕ namely the ordinate of the standard normal distribution (or, equivalently, the probability density of a standardized normal random variate), corresponding to a standard score of χ such that 0.20 of the distribution is above χ. χ here equals 0.84, meaning that in a normal distribution 20 per cent of the population have standardized scores above 0.84. The corresponding ϕ is 0.280. So, $\phi/\pi = 0.28/0.20 = 1.4$, meaning that the *average* Z_I in the selected group is 1.4.

15 *Market Signaling: Informational Transfer in Hiring and Related Screening Devices*, Harvard University Press, Cambridge, Mass., 1974, p. 80.

16 *Report on Secondary Education*, Board of Secondary Education, Lahore, 1956, p. 19.

17 'Examination System', *Pakistan Education Review*, No. 1, January 1970, p. 98.

18 'How Objective Are the Objective Tests?' *Pakistan Education Review*, No. 4, October 1970, p. 35.

19 Robert E. Klitgaard, *Making Merit Work: Selection for Higher Education in Developing Countries*, in press, chapter 2.

CHAPTER 8

A FACTOR ANALYSIS OF THE CONTRIBUTORS TO INFLATION IN PAKISTAN: 1960-75

Hafiz A. Pasha

Statistical analysis involves the careful marshalling of data—and the appreciation of those data's precise meaning. This chapter exemplifies the cautious appreciation of macro-economic data. It also applies the technique of factor analysis, in an exploratory effort to assess the sources of inflation.

Introduction

Economics has been called a dismal science and an exact science; but in many of its manifestations, it is at best a murky science, even when dealing with numbers. A case in point is the econometric analysis of inflation in Pakistan from 1960 to 1975.

Some facts were beyond dispute, even to non-economists. From 1972 to 1975, inflation averaged over 20 per cent a year. Over the previous twelve years, the average had been only about 3.5 per cent a year. The common man, no less than the policy maker and economist, was concerned about this rise. He wanted to know what caused it and what could be done about it.

Speculation about the causes was abundant. During the first half of the seventies, international inflationary forces were at work, and the rate of growth of the economy was relatively slow. The money supply expanded rapidly. Structural distortions appeared, as most of the growth was concentrated in the non-commodity producing sectors; incomes were redistributed in favour of lower income groups with a high propensity to consume. On top of all this, inflationary expectations may have given inflation a self-generating quality.

Presumably many of these phenomena affected inflation. From a policymaking perspective, the question was one of

---

This chapter was written by Hafiz A. Pasha.

degree: *how much* did each of the purported causes contribute to inflation? By discovering the degree to which different factors were operative, one might hope to make progress on the next policy question: how much could different policy alternatives contribute to the fight against inflation, and at what cost?

Unfortunately, little progress has been made in the quantitative assessment of the contribution of the different factors to inflation in Pakistan. This chapter, although neither definitive nor exact, represents an attempt at such assessment. If one could arrive, initially, at a ranking only of the importance of different factors in generating inflation, it would represent some progress on the quantitative front.

More broadly, this chapter shows how factor analysis— a statistical technique seldom used in economic research— might be used to analyse such a subject. We also identify some of the major shortcomings in 'real-world' empirical research on inflation in a country like Pakistan, including lack of appropriate and accurate data and the need for an estimation technique which is based on acceptable assumptions.

Choice of Variables

Attempts were made to include in the analysis all variables which were presumed, *a priori*, to have an impact on inflation. Constraints on the final choice were whether these variables were directly measurable (or had quantifiable proxies) and whether data were available from 1960 to 1975. These constraints eliminated 'inflationary expectations' as a variable, for no meaningful, quantifiable indicator was available. Crude indicators of expectations were rejected as passive reflectors of the actual path of inflation.[1] In order to quantify the effect of inflationary expectations on the rate of inflation, a system of surveys will have to be instituted to find out what different groups in the population expect the future rate of inflation to be, as is done, for instance, in the United Kingdom.[2]

After numerous explorations, we retained the following variables (Table 8.1).

Table 8.1
THE DATA
(percentages)

	Rate of inflation	Growth of money supply	Growth of money supply (lagged by one year)	Growth of import volume	Growth of import prices	Growth of export volume	Growth of export prices	Tax burden variable	Structural variable	Growth of real GDP
1960-1	3.8	4.2	5.4	13.0	3.5	-2.3	5.4	7.5	67.9	4.9
1961-2	-1.7	0.2	4.2	-4.3	8.9	-2.4	5.2	-2.3	24.8	6.3
1962-3	0.0	14.7	0.2	18.0	4.9	51.8	-8.8	-4.8	44.7	7.6
1963-4	5.4	11.1	14.7	4.9	1.9	-4.1	6.6	2.1	54.4	6.7
1964-5	4.4	9.6	11.1	21.8	-1.3	-0.2	2.0	10.0	52.9	8.6
1965-6	2.7	13.7	9.6	-16.5	0.3	4.4	18.5	-0.4	67.7	5.4
1966-7	9.4	9.7	13.7	18.1	5.0	5.9	5.2	18.7	25.8	3.8
1967-8	2.0	6.7	9.7	-2.7	-3.6	12.9	-2.8	-15.6	23.4	8.0
1968-9	0.2	9.5	6.7	-5.4	0.3	2.1	9.0	6.7	47.9	6.4
1969-70	4.0	10.6	9.5	2.7	5.1	3.5	1.5	0.0	42.8	9.3
1970-1	5.2	7.0	10.6	1.4	3.2	6.7	-4.4	-15.6	100.0*	0.1
1971-2	6.3	44.5	7.0	-22.1	5.8	0.8	-2.4	0.9	39.6	0.9
1972-3	15.2	27.1	44.5	13.6	104.0	20.8	98.2	12.5	70.6	7.3
1973-4	25.4	17.3	27.1	23.4	30.9	-10.6	33.0	-6.9	64.3	4.4
1974-5	22.3	11.7	17.3	19.6	31.1	-17.9	24.6	5.2	100.0*	2.6
1975-6	10.7	22.5	11.7	0.8	-5.1	8.7	0.3	8.7	50.5	4.8

Note: 'Structural variable' is in the percentage of incremental GDP accounted for by the non-commodity producing sector.
*In order not to get very large values, particularly for 1970-1, we have constrained the value of this variable to a maximum of 100.0. In the years when we assign this value it indicates that the increase in the value added in the services sector is greater than the increase in the total value added in the economy.
Source: See the statistical appendix, where all the variables are defined.

Growth of real GDP. Various hypotheses have been advanced regarding the nature of relationship between the rate of growth of the economy and the rate of inflation in developing countries. According to the 'structuralist' view, as an economy grows faster, bottlenecks of capacity appear in various sectors, which in turn trigger off price increases. The 'monetarists' emphasize that deficit financing, used to push up growth through a higher level of public investment, is likely to be inflationary, especially in the short run. Both schools postulate that there is a possible relationship between the rate of growth and the rate of inflation.

There is, however, a contrary view. Growth, particularly in the agricultural sector, improves the supply position of a number of commodities. By reducing the imbalance between demand and supply, this may lead to a lower rate of inflation. On the basis of this thinking, therefore, growth maybe inversely related to inflation. Our subsequent analysis will help us to assess this relationship historically in the Pakistani context.

Growth of money supply. We have used the strict definition of money supply, modified by certain simplifying assumptions. Strictly defined, money supply consists of currency in circulation and of demand liabilities of scheduled banks. Unfortunately, data on both these components were not available for West Pakistan alone. Therefore, a number of assumptions were made in order to arrive at the estimated annual growth rate of money supply between 1960-1 and 1974-5 as outlined in the statistical appendix at the end of the chapter.

Earlier studies of inflation in Pakistan have observed that monetary expansion appears to have an impact on prices with a certain time lag. Azhar[3] estimates this lag as being one year. We included two monetary variables in the analysis: the rate of growth of money supply in year t and in year t-1.

Hashmi and Faruqui[4] take as their monetary expansion variable the level of government deficit financing as a percentage of the GDP in current prices. Historically, the public sector has not been the only source of monetary expansion. Therefore, in order to get an overall view of the impact of monetary expansion on inflation, we have also included monetary expansion due to the foreign sector and the private sector.

Growth of import prices. We want to assess how changes in import prices—which reflect international inflation throughout the period and the devaluation in 1971—affect inflation. At the highly aggregated level at which the analysis is being done we have considered only the overall price trends of imports. A possible refinement would be to separate the price trends of imports of capital goods, raw materials, and finished consumer goods, in order to determine their individual impact. The intensity of inflationary impact of each type of import is likely to be different depending largely upon the degree of competition in the home market. This refinement would, therefore, highlight the difference in the quantitative contribution of the price trends of each type of import. At the aggregate level we have tried to determine the overall price trends of imports from international sources and from the former East Pakistan up to 1971. The method of construction of the combined price index is outlined in the statistical appendix.

Growth in the volume of imports. This variable has been included to assess how the liberalization of our import policy, particularly in the last three years, may have restrained inflationary pressures. Conversely, it may indicate the cost of quantitative restrictions of imports in terms of the higher inflation caused. This variable will help us to quantify the trade-off between conserving foreign exchange and controlling inflation. As in the case of prices, we have constructed a combined volume index of imports made internationally and from the former East Pakistan.

Growth of export prices. This variable measures another transmitter of international inflationary pressures into the domestic economy. Its quantitative contribution depends on how the prices of domestically consumed items that are also partly exported respond to changes in the export prices. Presumably, the market mechanism or government intervention ensures that any newly created differentials in profitability between selling in the foreign or in the home markets, due to changes in international prices, are at least partly removed through domestic price adjustments. Again, a combined export price index has been constructed of international exports and of exports to the former East Pakistan.[5]

Growth of the indirect tax burden. It has been asserted that one of the causes of inflation of prices in the manufacturing sector has been an increasing burden of indirect taxes on this sector. Efforts by governments to raise tax revenues on this basis have been considered to have inflationary implications. In order to test this hypothesis, we had to define a measure of tax burden. The base for taxation was taken as the value-added in the manufacturing sector at current factor cost (i.e., including indirect taxes such as import duties, excise duties, and sales tax). The yield from these taxes divided by the value-added gives the burden due to taxation. Further details are given in the statistical appendix.

Growth of structural imbalances. 'Structuralists' contend growth rates of different sectors are likely to diverge during the process of development. In particular, they identify agriculture as potentially the lagging sector. Incomes generated in the relatively fast-growing manufacturing sector are likely to spill over in the form of demand for food, thereby causing inflation in food prices. In Pakistan, growth rates of the manufacturing and the agricultural sectors have diverged at different times. In the highly inflationary 1970-5 period, however, both sectors were lagging; the primary stimulus for growth came from the service sector. In 1975, the service sector in Pakistan was roughly the same size as the agricultural sector and about twice the size of the manufacturing sector. Therefore, in terms of the overall inflationary impact, any divergence between the growth rate of the service sector and the growth rate of the commodity-producing sectors (agriculture and manufacturing) is of greater quantitative significance than the divergence between the growth rates of the manufacturing and the agricultural sectors. The choice of our structural imbalance variable reflects this view. It is defined for any year as the percentage of the incremental GDP accounted for by the increase in the value-added in the non-commodity producing sector (i.e., the service sector).

Rate of inflation. We have taken the rate of change in the 'implicit' GDP deflator as the measure of the rate of inflation. It is the most comprehensive indicator of inflation, as it allows for changes in the prices not only of commodities but also of services. The wholesale price index, the alternative indicator of inflation, is highly correlated (r = 0.97) with the deflator. Our results for the latter will, therefore, be more or less the same as for the former. As for the consumer price index, it has been constructed for all income groups in West Pakistan only from 1969 onwards; consequently, it could not be used in our analysis.

Using Factor Analysis

The technique of factor analysis was developed by psychologists and statisticians, particularly in connection with the analysis of mental factors from scores on various psychological tests. It has seldom been employed in economic studies. Adelman and Morris used factor analysis in several studies of developing countries, including their pioneering 1966 research on the social and political determinants of fertility.[6]

The primary purpose of factor analysis is to reduce a number of explanatory variables into a smaller number of independent factors, in terms of which the whole set of variables may be better understood. Each factor is a linear combination of all the explanatory variables. Specifically, each factor is an eigenvector of the correlation matrix of the original variables. The correlation matrix is given in Table 8.2.

Mathematically, the factors are formed in this way:

- Those variables that are most closely intercorrelated are combined into a single factor.
- The variables allocated to a given factor are those most nearly independent of those allocated to other factors.
- The factors are derived in a manner which maximizes the percentage of the total variance attributable to each successive factor (given the inclusion of the preceding factors).
- The factors are uncorrelated, in most forms of factor analysis including that used here.

Two types of factors can be distinguished. Common factors are those required to explain the intercorrelations among the variables. Unique factors account for that portion of variation of a particular variable which cannot be attributed to the correlation of the variable with other variables in the set. Each variable can be expressed as a linear composite of the common factors, a unique factor, and a random error. Factor analysis can, therefore, be interpreted as a regression of the observed variables on the unobserved common factors and the unique factor.

A major aim of factor analysis is to determine the coefficients relating the observed variables to the common factors. These coefficients are referred to as factor loadings. They play the same role in factor analysis as regression coefficients in multiple regression analysis. The squared factor loadings represent the relative contribution of each factor to the total standardized variance of a variable. The sum for each variable of its squared factor loadings gives the communality coefficient which is analogous to the coefficient of multiple determination ($\bar{R}^2$) in regression analysis.

The rotated factor matrix is the matrix of factor loadings, which not only indicates the importance of each factor in explaining the variables, but also provides the basis for grouping the variables into common factors. Each variable is allocated to that factor in which it has the highest loading—that factor with which it is most closely correlated.

Table 8.2
ZERO-ORDER CORRELATION COEFFICIENTS MATRIX
FOR THE TEN VARIABLES

	X_1	X_2	X_3	X_4	X_5	X_6	X_7	X_8	X_9	X_{10}
X_1	1.00	0.30	0.72	0.52	0.59	−0.41	0.57	0.15	0.50	−0.31
X_2	−	1.00	0.33	−0.29	0.38	0.12	0.32	0.09	0.02	−0.31
X_3	−	−	1.00	0.36	0.90	−0.12	0.93	0.28	0.34	0.04
X_4	−	−	−	1.00	1.32	0.05	0.25	0.33	0.24	0.22
X_5	−	−	−	−	1.00	0.10	0.96	0.30	0.32	0.06
X_6	−	−	−	−	−	1.00	−0.02	−0.14	−0.26	0.32
X_7	−	−	−	−	−	−	1.00	0.37	0.32	0.11
X_8	−	−	−	−	−	−	−	1.00	−0.07	0.19
X_9	−	−	−	−	−	−	−	−	1.00	−0.48
X_{10}	−	−	−	−	−	−	−	−	−	1.00

X_1 = Rate of inflation
X_2 = Growth of money supply
X_3 = Growth of money supply (lagged by one year)
X_4 = Growth of import volume
X_5 = Growth of import prices
X_6 = Growth of export volume
X_7 = Growth of export prices
X_8 = Tax burden variable
X_9 = Structural variable
X_{10} = Growth of real GDP

Table 8.3 gives the results of our factor analysis. The factors will be described shortly. To interpret the Table, observe that the first row of rotated factor matrix gives the loadings of each factor in explaining the variable which we are primarily interested in analysing. The squares of these loadings gives the extent of the variation explained by this factor. The last column of the matrix gives the communality coefficients, which measure the extent of variation in each variable that is explained by all common factors combined. (The rest of the variation can be attributed to the unique factor and random error.)

Why factor analysis instead of multiple regression analysis? Each technique has its advantages. In the case at hand for instance, we believed that factor analysis would prove illuminating, for several reasons. First, it permits a study of mutual

Table 8.3
ROTATED FACTOR MATRIX FOR THE TEN VARIABLES*

		Rotated factor loadings				Communality coefficient
		F_1	F_2	F_3	F_4	
1.	Rate of inflation	0.72	0.53	−0.16	−0.09	0.83
2.	Rate of growth of import prices	0.96	−0.08	0.04	0.05	0.94
3.	Rate of growth of export prices	0.94	−0.02	0.03	0.15	0.91
4.	Rate of expansion of money supply in t-1	0.94	0.09	−0.03	0.09	0.91
5.	Rate of growth of volume of exports	0.06	−0.88	0.05	−0.23	0.84
6.	Rate of growth of real GDP	0.00	−0.66	−0.37	0.47	0.80
7.	Structural variable	0.41	0.50**	−0.21	−0.54	0.76
8.	Rate of expansion of money supply	0.44	0.02	0.79	−0.01	0.82
9.	Rate of growth of volume of imports	0.41	0.02	−0.79	0.08	0.80
10.	Tax burden variable	0.30	0.15	−0.09	0.81	0.77

*Boxes indicate the factor to which each variable is assigned.
**The structural variable has nearly the same loading in factors 2 and 4. We have preferred to put it in factor 2 where it has the correct sign.

interdependence. Unlike regression analysis, it does not presume that the direction of effects is from the 'independent' variables to the 'dependent' variable.

Second, if the variables are highly intercorrelated, factor analysis will combine them into a single factor. In contrast, multiple regression analysis faces a number of statistical difficulties if the independent variables are highly correlated. In our data set, for example, the rates of growth of import prices and of export prices were highly correlated (r = 0.96). International inflation apparently had a simultaneous impact on import and export prices. It would be awkward to assume, as regression analysis would do, that export prices remained constant while import prices varied. Factor analysis neatly solves this problem. First it bunches variables that are closely related into separate factors. Then it tests for the significance of each factor by holding the other factors constant. A factor analysis of our data will bunch import prices and the export prices together in the same factor.

Findings

Our results are shown in Table 8.3. Factor 1 explains 51.8 per cent (=0.72^2 x 100) of the variation in the rate of inflation. Factor 2 explains 28.1 per cent, and an additional 3.4 per cent is attributable to factors 3 and 4. The total variation in the rate of inflation explained by these four factors is 83.3 per cent. How might we interpret each factor?

Factor 1. Three variables have their highest loadings in this factor: the rate of growth of import prices, the rate of growth of export prices, and the rate of growth of money supply in the previous year. This factor may be thought of as summarizing the effect of international inflation and domestic monetary expansion on the price level. It is clearly the most significant factor.

Notice that the factor analysis bunched together variables showing the effect of international inflation and domestic monetary expansion. These variables are highly correlated. As shown in Table 8.2, the values of r_{35} and r_{37} are 0.90 and 0.93 respectively. Since international inflation and domestic monetary expansion have exercised their maximum impact

on inflation at the same time, it is not possible to isolate
their individual contribution. But since 51.8 per cent of the
variation in the rate of inflation can be ascribed to this factor,
we reckon that half or more of the variation in inflation in
Pakistan from 1960 to 1975 can not be explained by
international factors.

Factor 2. Three variables are closely associated with it:
the rate of growth of real GDP, the rate of growth of the
volume of exports, and the percentage of the incremental
growth in the economy accounted for by the non-commodity
producing sector. This factor seems to summarize the effect
of growth and its composition on the rate of inflation in the
economy.

An examination of the signs of the loadings of the different
variables in this factor has interesting implications. The
growth of real GDP has a negative sign, which indicates that
in the Pakistani context the faster growth of the economy
has meant a lower rate of inflation. This contrasts with the
hypotheses presented by many 'structuralists' and 'monetarists'.
An improved supply position for various commodities seems
to have exercised a more powerful downward pressure on
the rate of inflation than the upward push on prices exerted
by the emergence of structural bottlenecks or of deficit
financing used for development purposes.

The sign of the growth of the volume of exports variable
is also negative. This is an interesting result. It indicates that
faster growth in volume of exports did not lead to a higher
rate of inflation. Increases in the export of various commodities did not seem to come at the expense of domestic consumption but through higher production.

The sign of the structural variable is positive, as expected.
As most of the growth of the economy tended to become
concentrated in the non-commodity producing sector, it
resulted in some 'structural' inflation. But the quantitative
contribution of this structural element to inflation was not
very great. Its factor loading of 0.50 was the smallest of the
three variables in factor 2.

Factor 3. This factor, which explains about 2.6 per cent of
the variation in the rate of inflation, bunches two variables:
the rate of growth of money supply and the rate of growth of

the volume of imports. The latter has a negative sign. This indicates that import liberalization does exercise some restraining effect, though marginal, on inflation.

Factor 4. This factor, mostly reflecting the tax burden variable, explains only 0.8 per cent of the variation in inflation. Variations in indirect taxation in the manufacturing sector did not appear to have much of an impact on the overall rate of inflation.

About 16.7 per cent of the variation in the rate of inflation was not explained by the four factors. Perhaps this part of the variation may be attributed to the effect of variables that we could not include in our analysis, such as wage increases, income redistribution, inflationary expectations, and others, as well as to random error.

Conclusions

Our results indicate that at most half the inflation experienced by Pakistan over the period 1960 to 1975 can be ascribed to international factors. The scope for domestic policy action to reduce the rate of inflation was probably greater than the pronouncements of many government officials might have led us to believe. Our results indicate that restraint of the rate of domestic monetary expansion is likely to be an effective anti-inflationary device, although the impact of prices is lagged by one year. It also seems that faster growth of production has a significant anti-inflationary impact. Although faster growth may generate 'structural' inflation, the improvement in supply position of a number of commodities particularly in the agricultural sector actually reduces the element of 'demand-pull' inflation in finished consumer goods. On a net basis, the impact on inflation is downwards.

The findings also confirm that the composition of growth in the economy matters from the viewpoint of inflation. If faster growth of the services sector is encouraged as part of a programme for achieving greater social justice, this may have to be traded off with additional inflation that is caused. If the additional inflation generated has a regressive impact on real incomes, then such an approach to achieving greater equity may be partly self-defeating in the end.

The approach of this chapter could be extended and refined in many ways. One might analyse variables at a more disaggregated level. An immediate extension that suggests itself is the study of inflation in agricultural and industrial prices separately. By this extension a greater insight may be had in the relative success of different anti-inflationary policies in the two sectors.

STATISTICAL APPENDIX

The principal sources of data were *25 Years of Pakistan in Statistics* and *Pakistan Economic Survey, 1974-5,* published by the Central Statistical Division and the Economic Advisers' Wing, Islamabad. Additional sources had to be consulted in some cases. These sources along with the methods of estimation used are outlined as follows:

Growth of real GDP. The reporting system of the National Income Accounts was significantly improved in 1969-70. The value-added due to certain activities, such as Pakistan International Airlines, was reported for the first time. Consequently, the growth rate of the economy between 1968-9 and 1969-70 was over 18 per cent. It was necessary to remove the downward bias in the GDP figures prior to 1969-70. Fortunately, data on the GDP, calculated on the basis of the practice that had been in existence since 1969-70 was available in the April 1972 issue of the *Statistical Bulletin.* These data permitted the calculation of the 'improvement factor' in the sectors where there had been a once-and-for-all jump in value-added in 1969-70 due to the improvement in the reporting system. The value-added figures of these sectors between 1959-60 and 1968-9 were accordingly adjusted. By this method, the downward bias in the GDP figures prior to 1969-70 was removed. The annual growth rate of the economy was then calculated.

Growth of money supply. As mentioned in the text, data on currency in circulation and demand deposits were not available separately for West Pakistan. For the period December 1960-70, however, Rabbani and Repetto estimated the currency in circulation in the former East Pakistan.[7] Since data on currency in circulation in undivided Pakistan is available, we were able to arrive at the figures for West Pakistan. As our analysis has been carried out on a financial year basis, it was necessary to get estimates of currency in circulation at the end of June of each year. This was done by taking a two-year moving average of the December figures. Total bank deposits, demand plus time, in West Pakistan during the period June 1961-71 are given in *Banking Statistics,* published by the State Bank of Pakistan. Since data on bank deposits in the whole of undivided Pakistan are also available, it was possible to calculate the share of West Pakistan in total deposits for each year. Assuming that in each year West Pakistan's share of demand deposits was as its share of total deposits, we estimated the demand deposits in West Pakistan from June 1961-71. We estimated the demand deposits in East Pakistan at the end of June 1971 to be Rs 1,581.7 million. This figure was excluded from the demand deposits figures after June 1971 to give the demand deposits in West Pakistan from June 1971 onwards.[8]

Growth of import prices. A unit value index of imports from East Pakistan never appears to have been constructed, and we were faced with the task of constructing one. Our source of data on interwing trade was *25 Years of Pakistan in Statistics.* Unfortunately, the data on interwing trade appears to be subject to a fairly substantial margin of error. In particular, the unit values of individual commodity imports fluctuate widely from year to year. In some years for some commodities, data were not provided on the quantity imported; in such cases, we had to resort to crude interpolation. We decided to concentrate on the price trends of the principal imports only and assume an overall price trend for the remainder of the imports. Accordingly, separate indices were constructed for imports of matches, paper, tea, and jute bags. The base year was taken as 1960-1 to correspond with the base year of international imports. These four items accounted for 7.3 per cent, 10.8 per cent, 30.2 per cent, and 9.4 per cent, respectively, of the total value of imports in 1960-1. Their combined contribution was 57.7 per cent. For the rest of the imports, which consisted of a motley collection of commodities, we took the general wholesale price index (converted to the 1960-1 base by splicing) in the former East Pakistan as representative of their collective price trend. After constructing this unit value index we combined it with the international imports unit value index by taking the weights corresponding to the share of the commodity or group of commodities in total interwing imports of West Pakistan in 1960-1.

Growth of volume of imports. Separate volume indices were constructed by finding out the total rupee value of international imports from 1959-60 to 1974-5 and converting these figures into index form by using the value of imports in 1960-1 as the base of 100. The value of imports index was divided by the unit value index of international imports, given in the *Pakistan Economic Survey,* and multiplied by 100. The resulting figures correspond to the volume index of imports with 1960-1 as base year.

The volume index of interwing imports during the period 1959-60 to 1971-2 was constructed in a similar manner. The total value of imports from the former East Pakistan were converted into index form and divided by the unit value index that we constructed. An overall volume index of imports was created by using weights proportional to the value of imports internationally and from the former East Pakistan in 1960-1. This system of weights was used for the period 1959-60 to 1970-1. From 1971-2 onwards, the unit value index of international imports became the overall unit value index. It is possible that the change of weights may have affected our estimate of growth in import prices in the year they were changed, 1971-2.

Growth of export prices. As in the case of import prices, we were confronted with the task of constructing a unit value index of exports of West Pakistan to the former East Pakistan. We resorted to a similar approach to the one adopted for estimating the unit value index of imports. Principal exports were identified. These were rice, rape and mustard seed, cotton yarn, and cotton cloth. Their respective shares of total exports in 1960-1 were 6.9 per cent, 10.5 per cent, 17.1 per cent, and 17.0 per cent. Their combined share was 51.6 per cent. For the other exports, it was assumed that their collective price trend corresponded to the wholesale price index (converted to 1960-1 base by splicing) in West Pakistan.

The rest of the procedure was identical to that done in constructing the import unit value index.

Growth of export volume. The method of estimation was again similar to that used for constructing the overall volume index of imports.

Growth of indirect tax burden. The yield of the indirect taxes—import duties, excise duties and sales tax—in West Pakistan were taken from Akhlaqur Rehman,[9] who gives the receipt figures for the period 1960-1 to 1969-70. In order to arrive at an estimate of the yield of the different taxes for the years 1959-60 and 1970-1 it was assumed that the yield of a tax in West Pakistan as a percentage of the overall all-Pakistan yield was the same as that for the nearest year for which information is available. It was assumed that the tax receipts from the former East Pakistan in 1971-2 was about one-sixth of the total yield in 1970-1. This enabled estimation of the tax receipts from West Pakistan in 1971-2.

NOTES

[1] For example, it may be assumed that expectations about future price increases are likely to be based on past experience. In particular, the rate of inflation expected in the coming year might be taken as some weighted average of the rate of inflation in previous years. The weights could be constructed in such a manner that greater importance is attached to the most recent experience with price increases and successively decreasing weight to the rate of inflation going back in time. The standard example of an expectations variable, r_t^e, which has these properties is:

$$r_t^e = \frac{1}{\lambda-1} \Sigma (\frac{1}{\lambda})^n P_{t-n}, \quad \lambda > 1.$$

Other measures of expectations were also formulated. When the expectations variable, r_t^e, was included in our analysis, it explained most of the variance in the rate of inflation, and most of the other variables appeared to behave perversely (i. e., they had the wrong sign). Therefore, we deigned it necessary to exclude this variable from our analysis.

[2] J. A. Carlson and M. Parkin, 'Inflation Expectations', *Economica*, Vol. 42, No. 166, May 1975.

[3] B. A. Azhar, 'An Econometric Analysis of Price Behaviour in Pakistan', *Pakistan Development Review*, Vol. XIII, No. 4 Winter 1973.

[4] S. A. Hashmi and A. Faruqui, 'Some Causative Factors of Inflation in Pakistan', paper presented at a seminar at the Administrative Staff College, Lahore, September 1974.

[5] We have several variables on the foreign sector of the economy. It has been suggested that an alternative measure of imported inflation could be the 'openness' of the economy defined as the size of the foreign trade sector or the sum of imports plus exports divided by the gross national product. This

measure has the obvious merit of simplicity. But the same change in 'openness' may lead to widely different changes in the rate of inflation. In fact, it is possible that sometimes an increase in openness would lead to a higher rate of inflation and in other cases to a lower rate of inflation. The former outcome might occur if the change were caused by a rise in import prices; the latter if the increase in imports were caused by an increase in the volume of imports, prices remaining unchanged. We have, therefore, sacrificed simplicity for measures that show price and volume effects separately. An additional justification for this choice: the government and other bodies often quote the phenomenal rates of increase in prices of major imported items—such as fuel, food, fertilizers, and edible oil—as demonstrating that inflation is imported. Official explanations have not been carried out in terms of the increase of the size of the foreign trade sector relative to the economy. Our analysis has the advantage of allowing us to follow the distinction.

[6] I. Adelman and C. T. Morris, 'A Quantitative Study of the Social and Political Determinants of Fertility', *Economic Development and Cultural Change*, Vol. XIV, No. 2, January 1966.

[7] A. K. M. G. Rabbani and R. C. Repetto, 'Foodgrains Availability, Money Supply, and Price Level in East Pakistan: Some Simple Econometrics on Short-term Stabilizing Policies', *Pakistan Development Review*, Vol. XIII, No. 2, Summer 1968.

[8] Our method of estimation may inflate the share of West Pakistan in demand deposits in June 1971, because West Pakistan's share of demand deposits was lower and its share of time deposits higher than its share of total deposits. In June 1972, after deducting the amount of Rs 1,581.70 million from the overall demand deposits figure, we get a level of demand deposits in West Pakistan that is 52.1 per cent higher than June 1971. Therefore, the overall rates of monetary expansion in 1971-2 comes out as 44.5 per cent, which, we suspect, is biased upwards. We did not know how to correct for this anomaly.

[9] N. A. Rehman, *The Structure of Taxation in Pakistan*, UBL Research Monographs, No. 4, June 1972.